HEALTH & WG

yoga

This is a FLAME TREE book
First published 2013

Publisher and Creative Director: Nick Wells
Senior Project Editors: Sara Robson & Catherine Taylor
Copy Editor: Anna Groves
Picture Research: Emma Chafer
Art Director: Mike Spender
Photographer: Alexandra Hunt
Photography Director: Charmaine Yabsley

Acknowledgements

The publishers would like to thank Donna Abbate, yoga instructor and program manager at Gwinganna Health Retreat. Her generosity with her time and poses, whilst we photographed her over and over again, meant that this book was a joy to write and photograph. Many thanks Donna.

We would also like to thank Gwinganna Health Retreat for allowing us to shoot the beautiful photographs featured in this book. Despite torrential rain, we still managed to catch the yogic essence! For more information on Gwinganna Health Retreat, visit www.gwinganna.com

Many thanks also to Alexandra Hunt, for her wonderful and inspired photography.

Many thanks to Yoga Matters (www.yogamatters.com) for supplying several images (see below).

Publisher's Note:

All reasonable care has been exercised by the author and publisher to ensure that the advice and poses included in this guide are safe. However, it is still important to note that this guide is not intended as a complete substitute for instruction from a qualified yoga teacher and all poses should be attempted with caution. Neither the editors, the author nor the publisher take responsibility for any injury sustained when using this book.

This edition first published 2013 by
FLAME TREE PUBLISHING
6 Melbray Mews
Fulham, London SW6 3NS
United Kingdom

www.flametreepublishing.com

ISBN 978-0-85775-817-0

A CIP record for this book is available from the British Library upon request.

The author has made all reasonable efforts to ensure that the information in this book is correct at the time of going to print, and the publishers cannot accept any liability for incorrect or out-of-date information. The publisher would be glad to rectify any omissions in future editions of this book.

Printed in China

Photographs © Flame Tree Publishing Ltd except the below.
Courtesy of and © www.yogamatters.com: 47b, 48cb, 48t, 48b, 55b.
Courtesy of Shutterstock.com and © the following photographers: yuriy kulik 4 & 16; VetrovaMaria 5b & 52; wavebreakmedia 5t & 30; EpicStockMedia 6t & 190; VaclavHroch 6b & 216; Pressmaster 7c & 230, 8; Christopher Edwin Nuzzaco 9b; StockLife 9t; ingret 10b & 54; Anna Furman 11b; Robert Kneschke 11t, 22t, 222b, 240c; Markus Gann 12t; iofoto 12b, 15c; zstock 13t; Pete Saloutos 14c; Yuri Arcurs 18b; Alexander Tihonov 19b; Yellowj 19t; dean sanderson 20t, 209b; Pikoso.kz 20b, 27c, 100c, 159t, 226c, 237b, 238c; MANDY GODBEHEAR 21b; Malakhova Ganna 22b; BasPhoto 23b; Bishwambers Photography 23t; Andrey Plis 24c; noppharat 25c; Henk Paul 26c; Nejron Photo 28c; Goodluz 32c; Lucky Business 35t; T-Design 36t; Elena Ray 37b, 233t; BestPhotoStudio 38b; oksix 38t; Aleksandr Doodko 39t; holbox 39t; AnneMS 40b; Buida Nikita Yourievich 41t; Andresr 43b; Andrey_Popov 45c; Andrei Zarubaika 46t; Venus Angel 47t; Brooke Becker 48c; NataliTerr 49; Africa Studio 50; DiscoDad 163b; Stephen Orsillo 145t; Miljan Mladenovic 150b; Deklofenak 154t, 161t, 179t; Anthony Maragou 208b; piotr maicinski 210b; caimacanul 211b; Gravicapa 212c; Ana Blazic Pavlovic 213b; Kzenon 214c; Sergey Mironov 218b; Ramona Heim 219b; Bevan Goldswain 220b; Piotr Marcinski 221c; Michelangelo Gratton 232b; Pinkcandy 234b; FikMik 235t; sergei telegin 235b; Artur Bogacki 237t; dean bertoncelj 241t; Photo Dreamers 242c; marcstock 243t; Rido 243b; stefanolunardi 244c.

HEALTH & WELLBEING

yoga

Charmaine Yabsley & David Smith

Foreword by Martin Clark,
Editor of OM Yoga & Lifestyle magazine

**FLAME TREE
PUBLISHING**

Contents

Yoga offers so much that, after reading this chapter, you may regard it as not just a workout, but a way of life. It not only calms the mind but also improves flexibility, strength and physical performance. Learn all about the history of this ancient discipline, illustrating how yoga has evolved from its 4,000-year-old roots, and get to grips with the practice's six main paths, including Bhakti, Hatha and Mantra yoga. Practising yoga helps to create a stillness of the mind, which, together with meditation and breathing exercises, focuses your outlook and does wonders for your health!

Getting Ready

Yoga is suitable for anyone, regardless of age, shape or size, and is perfect to ease stress, improve circulation and restore health. This section takes you through a host of factors important when beginning your yoga journey, such as the different styles of yoga, some of which can be more gruelling than others, whilst giving you practical tips on finding a class that suits you, your level and ability. The chapter also provides advice on how to incorporate yoga into your everyday life, as well as useful information on what to wear, what equipment to use and what diet to follow.

The Postures

There are so many yoga poses that it may seem daunting to know where to begin, but this chapter takes you through all the 'asanas' step by step, with tips to ensure maximum achievement and minimum pain. Each subsection guides you through specific types of poses, gradually becoming more difficult as each section progresses. So don't worry if you can't achieve a downward facing dog or a headstand on your first go – the most important thing with yoga is to begin gradually and calmly and do what is right for you.

Developing Your Practice

This section does exactly what it says and aims to develop your practice of yoga, by directing you through specific sequences, including warm-up sequences designed to introduce yoga to the beginner and ease your body into a session. There are also sequences for the more advanced yoga student, designed to challenge both body and mind. The chapter also provides advice on some of the difficulties and restrictions of yoga, including reassurance that yoga is about personal development, and not a race. Yoga has great health benefits, and the end of this chapter lists common ailments that yoga practice may help to improve.

Breath Control

Breathing technique is as much a part of yoga practice as the asanas themselves. Properly practised, breathing exercises can make you calmer, more peaceful, and reenergized. Breathing is a direct link between you, your body and the outside world. Known as 'pranayama' (the art of controlling the breath), this chapter explores the important relationship between yoga and breathing, including breathing exercises such as Bellows Breath, Alternate Nostril Breathing and the interestingly named Skull Shining Breath, to help you find peace, gain balance or cool down. This section acts as a perfect go-to guide when life's physical and emotional stresses get too much.

Meditation

Meditating is a fantastic way to de-stress and clear your mind in order to reduce anxiety, create an emotional balance and achieve life goals. This chapter sets you on your way to meditating correctly, with tips and advice on where to meditate, what to wear and the classic seated postures to adopt. The rest of the chapter concentrates on the different types of meditation, such as Mindfulness Meditation, which helps you learn to simply 'be', and Mantra Meditation, which focuses on chanting a sound or word. Don't be put off by the names, as all types of meditation are aimed at creating a stillness of the mind, so just find the technique that is best for you!

Foreword

If everyone did yoga, then the world would be a much better place. A bold statement, perhaps, but it's hard to imagine world leaders, or even school bullies, doing half the things they do after spending an hour or so chilling out on the mat – whether that's invading a Third World country or thumping you at break time for not handing over your sweets.

And the beauty of yoga is that anybody can do it. You are never too overweight or too old to start. The most important thing, as any instructor will tell you, is that you simply do it.

The yoga mat is a great leveller in so many ways. A place where you can not only throw a few shapes on the mat – no matter how awkward, or clumsy, at first – but where you get the space for some close introspection, for a quiet mind, for blissful relaxation.

The thing about yoga – this weird and wonderful discipline with its roots in ancient India – is that it benefits not only the body, but it also instills a great sense of peace and compassion within the practitioner. This inner calm comes after paying close personal attention to your body on the mat, especially your breathing – a vital and dynamic flowing link between you and the world around you – and quieting your mind's chatter. Quelling the rebellion inside your head is one of the great gifts of yoga and meditation and why it is so strongly recommended by doctors all over the world for relaxation and stress relief.

This greater sense of calm and wellbeing transmits into a new and profound understanding, not only of the self – both mentally and physically – but also one's place in the bigger picture. Yoga creates a vibrancy within, and this energy outwardly projects. After a while, others will pick up on your radiant yoga glow; smile and the world smiles with you, as the saying goes.

So, if everyone – and I mean everyone, right from the President down – took up yoga, there'd be a lot less fighting in the world and an awful lot more peace, love and understanding. I'm not saying we'd all be blissed-out all of the time – nothing would get done, for starters, which would be exceedingly annoying when your boiler breaks down – but wouldn't life be great if all our neighbours just said hello, for instance, or if kindly gents tipped their hats on their way to work?

Of course, if you're just looking for a quick workout to tone up your abs, then yoga offers that too. It's arguably the best workout there is – 4,000 years' worth of dedicated yogis can't be wrong, can they? But there is oh, so much more to it than that.

Yoga is a journey, from the first gentle moves in your beginners' class, to a greater empathy for all those around you. Stick with it, and you can end up with a fabulous Hollywood A-lister body. And if you're really committed, yoga will genuinely change your life.

This book is the perfect guide to help you get started on that journey.

Martin Clark
Editor of *OM Yoga &
Lifestyle* magazine

Introduction

A 4,000-year-old discipline from ancient India, these days, yoga can be all things to all people. First brought to the West in the late nineteenth century, it has been popularized in more recent years by celebrities such as pop icon Madonna, and other Hollywood stars, showcasing the bendy shapes and physical prowess yoga can help to create. Actually, yoga brings together a whole host of mental and spiritual benefits, as well as physical, though in the West it is now predominantly the health benefits derived from the exercises – or asanas – on the mat that appeal. For some, it's a weekly exercise routine; for others, a way of life.

Yoga, Yoga, Yoga

It may have originated in the East, but yoga is now everywhere in the West. As a means of keeping fit, there are classes pretty much anywhere you look. And they come in all shapes and sizes too: from gentle beginners' classes to high-octane, body-pumping Hot Yoga. Its beauty is its simplicity, even if you're not making particularly aesthetic shapes on the mat. Starting with a regular practice led by a qualified instructor at a local studio, it's easy to progress to a simple home practice which – with a bit of dedication – you can incorporate into your daily routine.

More than a Mat

But yoga is much more than just a weekly exercise class. The yoga lifestyle brings with it a huge range of other benefits, from calming meditation and spiritual enlightenment, through to healthier eating choices and a generally more conscious and present attitude to the world around you. The beauty of yoga is you can take from it just what you need. If all you want is a flat tummy, that's fine, but if you're searching for the meaning of life, yoga's not a bad place to start either.

Easy In

Find a class, get yourself there and just follow as best you can what your teacher is saying. Yoga is readily accessible, it can be as gentle – or as energetic – as you choose, and you'll probably meet lots of like-minded friends along the way. These days, yoga is everywhere, not some niche reserved for the ashrams of India, so it makes a great way to get yourself active and improve your lifestyle. Your first class may be quite an experience, especially if you don't know any of the postures, but nothing countless others haven't been through before. Tell your teacher if you're nervous.

The Benefits of Yoga

The huge benefits of yoga are covered in detail elsewhere in this book, but here's a brief summary for starters.

- **Feel-good factor**: Many yogis almost float out after a class, such is the mood-enhancing combination of exercise and relaxation on offer.

- **Stress free**: There are few things in life better for de-stressing the body and mind than yoga.

- **Any time, any place**: One of the greatest things about yoga is that, once you know a few simple moves or routines, or breathing exercises, you can take it wherever you go.

- **Be the change**: The yoga lifestyle can bring about deeper, more personal changes as well, including a more compassionate view of the world around you.

- **Money saver**: Yoga classes are not always cheap, especially if you're attending regularly, but if you can commence a home practice, then you'll save on costly gym memberships.

Chill out: Meditation and pranayama, or breathing exercises, are both fantastic ways of taking the edge off stressful life situations.

Flexibility: You may not be very bendy when you start, but, if you stick with it, yoga gets you twisting and turning the way nature intended, bit by bit.

Growing old gracefully: Yoga is the perfect tonic for more mature students to stay nimble and keep their full range of movement for longer.

Spiritual enlightenment: Yoga does not have to be spiritual at all, but many Western students who may have lost connection with organized religion find that it can spark a new interest in life's deeper meanings.

Being sociable: Make it to a regular class and you're bound to meet like-minded people; even online, there are countless places for the world's yoga community to connect.

About this Guide

This book is an ideal place for new yogis to discover more about what yoga is and all the wonderful things that it can lead to. It's perfect for those just starting out on the yogic path as well as those that may have already been to some classes and are looking to develop their practice a little more. Even the more experienced yogi will find something of interest.

In Class

Sometimes, you may discover in a class that instructors tell you how to do exercises in different ways. The fact is each teacher has their own style and brings with them their own unique background and range of experiences. Postures and breathing exercises will vary slightly from one teacher to another, just as every single person – and their physical body – is also unique. It's all yoga; just enjoy the ride.

Just Do It

The most important thing in your yoga practice is that you simply show up. If you don't go, or you don't do it, then you're only cheating yourself. Get to your class, or roll out your mat at home, and get down to work, no matter how light and easy your workout may be. A regular yoga practice is worth so much more than a quick flurry of classes and then nothing. Remember, the benefits are not just improved flexibility but also deep relaxation, calm and stress relief, and these things all take time.

Get Your Kit On

For the newcomer, the world of props and blocks can be confusing, but buying yoga kit does not have to be difficult – or expensive. Most classes – but not all – supply basic yoga mats, so you don't really need anything at first, just some loose, comfortable clothing. When you know yoga is something you wish to pursue longer term, then there is a huge choice when it comes to clothing, mats and other accessories. This book will help you keep costs down when you're starting out.

Fit for Life

Yoga is perhaps the greatest longevity tonic there is, a wholesome blend of physical exercise, healthier eating, mental relaxation and spiritual thoughtfulness. Get to know yourself better, inside and out.

Step It Up

If you do master the basic moves in class, then do look to develop a simple home practice. It's a cheap and easy way of feeling the benefits of yoga on a daily basis. Push yourself, but only if it feels right in your body. Experiment with other yoga styles; your body will love you for it.

Stay Safe

Yoga is great for your all-round health, but always listen to your body. Stretching can be challenging but it shouldn't be painful, so back off if there is discomfort. Qualified yoga teachers study anatomy so they can guide you, but if you're really concerned about anything, seek a doctor's advice.

Most importantly, whatever yoga you do, or whatever class you attend, it should always be fun. Keep that in mind when your teacher asks you to contort yourself into a shape that you haven't achieved since you were a five-year-old. So don't beat yourself up if you can't even touch your toes yet, or even see them. Yoga is fun; it's not competitive.

Yoga Basics

What Is Yoga?

The word *yoga* comes from the Sanskrit *yui*, which means 'to yoke' or 'to join' (Sanskrit is the ancient language of India, where yoga originated). This signifies the central theme of yoga – the union of body and mind, and ultimately, with the self and the universe. It's all about making connections, taking the student to a state of oneness, beyond their ego, and on to a new platform of expanded consciousness. Yoga is not just a workout, it's a way of life.

State of Mind

While yoga is commonly perceived in the West as a form of exercise (which it can be), regular practice can bring benefits and changes on multiple levels. While great attention is paid to the physical postures – called asanas – yoga can bring you more than just a great body. This ancient discipline helps practitioners look inward to find space and calm in their mind, through asana practice and also through meditation and breathing exercises (pranayama). This cultivates a greater awareness not only of the self, but also the individual's place in and connection to the world and cosmos.

Stilling the Mind

For many people, the cultivation of a peaceful mental and emotional state can be a wonderful benefit of yoga. This can bring relaxation and relief from stress. A regular yoga practice

allows the mind to mature, to transcend the ordinary external world of jobs, money and other mundane affairs, into a new healthy space. Yoga is also a means for body and mind to connect with the present moment, to wipe away thoughts about the past or fears for the future. This stilling of the mind, quelling the constant chatter of thoughts, is one reason many take up yoga.

Yoga is Union

Yoga's reputation as a physical practice is not without good reason. Dedicated and disciplined yoga practitioners can enjoy improved flexibility, strength and physical performance. But yoga, through asana and other disciplines, builds a bridge between the body and the mind, creating better balance. This is achieved through meditation, pranayama and many other aspects of the yoga lifestyle. With a calm and balanced mind, yoga can link the individual (body and mind) to a broader level of consciousness.

Top Tip

Yoga can unite body, mind and soul to create better balance in your life: not bad for an hour or so on the mat.

The Six Main Paths

Yoga is based on an ancient and holistic system, a practice that features six main paths. These are: Bhakti Yoga, Hatha Yoga, Jnana Yoga, Karma Yoga, Mantra Yoga and Raja Yoga.

Bhakti Yoga

Bhakti is a spiritual path of yoga, a discipline centred on love and devotion. This yogic path is founded on a longing to merge with the divine, to eliminate the ego and to surrender totally to God. It is a spiritual practice, without some of the other, more physical aspects of yoga, such as Hatha. In Bhakti, all is a manifestation of the divine; consequently, all else, including all material things and the ego, is meaningless. Bhakti is the most direct method to merge with the great universal consciousness.

Hatha Yoga

Hatha Yoga is a term you'll encounter everywhere, commonly used to describe generic physical yoga posture classes. In fact, it is one of the six yogic paths, but the one focused on perfecting the physical body, a pursuit aimed at bringing balance between mind and body, and developing greater consciousness. This is the yoga with which most people are familiar, working on flexibility, strength and suppleness to improve the body (*hatha* means 'forceful' in Sanskrit), and incorporating breathing techniques, relaxation and meditation. Most yoga classes will, ultimately, be some form of Hatha Yoga.

Did You Know?

There are six main yogic paths: Hatha Yoga is the most common type of yoga performed throughout the West today.

Jnana Yoga

This is the path of knowledge or discernment. The main aim of this path is to connect the finite self with the infinite cosmic consciousness. This is achieved through wisdom and knowledge, by withdrawing the mind and emotions, and plugging into the universal spirit, developing the ability to differentiate real from unreal. This yoga is about using your mind to achieve a higher state of consciousness, where the devotee experiences unity with God by freeing himself or herself from ignorance. Students must integrate the lessons of the other yogic paths before practising Jnana Yoga.

Karma Yoga

This is the yoga of action, or selfless service. In Karma Yoga, students are encouraged to act selflessly, to give everything, with nothing expected in return. It teaches students to release any ego, to detach themselves from the fruits of their actions, and to offer them instead to the

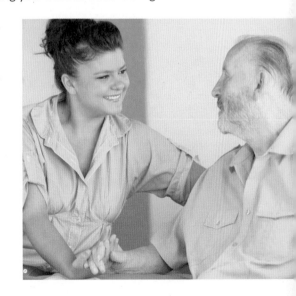

divine. The action itself is important, but so too is the way in which it is performed. These self-transcending actions, and the pathway of righteous living, help free the yogi from any karmic reactions, and bring them closer to God.

Mantra Yoga

Mantra Yoga is the yoga of chanting. Mantras are words or phrases or sounds that can be repeated over and over, with growing attention, and chanted thoughtfully. They are commonly used in meditations to overcome mind activity, and can also carry powerful spiritual messages, or even be used in the pursuit of personal transformation. The use of the mantra allows the yoga student to transcend mental activity and emotions to achieve a higher state of consciousness.

Raja Yoga

Raja Yoga is also known as the Great Yoga, or Classical Yoga, and includes elements of other pathways, such as Mantra and Hatha. This science of the mind is based on achieving awakening and ultimately enlightenment through meditation, stilling the mind and good health. This is why it is important to pursue Hatha Yoga before exploring other deeper, more spiritual yoga avenues.

The History of Yoga

The search for truth has generated diverse practices and disciplines that can be traced as far back as 1,800–1,000 BC with the Vedic epoch. Hence, yoga is often referred to as a 4,000-year-old discipline (although there is evidence that the fundamentals of yoga and meditation may have existed in the prehistoric era). Although yoga is seen in many countries, India stands out as the culture that brought completion to this pursuit of truth and oneness.

Historical Yoga Texts

Throughout the various historical epochs, there is evidence of sacred texts, teachings of mystics and gurus that systemized yoga and meditation. These texts are important for those looking to deepen their understanding of yoga.

Mahabharata

Starting with the Vedic epoch, we have the Mahabharata, originally written in Sanskrit. It is a beautifully written poem of over 100,000 verses, telling a grand and detailed story of two warring clans. The stories are filled with strife, battles and conflicts, and the descriptions are colourful and mesmerizing. The earliest stories were performed in the oral tradition and are still

being performed and retold as plays, in poetry, recitations and even movies. The messages contained are deep-rooted yogic philosophy, the main one being that beyond strife and conflict, exist transcendence and bliss.

The Upanishads

Moving forward, the next historical era to reveal a great sacred text was the Upanishadic epoch (800–500 BC). The Upanishads are mystical writings that share the technical teachings of many spiritual masters and saints, who were concerned with revealing methods of how to transcend. The scriptures were radical and came from an eclectic collection of sages,

offering a clear path to enlightenment. Today, they are still studied and continue to inspire many seekers on the path to truth. The relevant part here is the Yoga-Upanishad, which includes a vast amount of yoga instruction.

Bhagavad Gita

The Bhagavad Gita came into existence during the Gita epoch (500 BC–AD 200), and shows the beginning of the systemization of the basic technology of self-transcendence. This is a sacred scripture that shares the message that, beyond all attachment to life and its actions, there is only love and being. It is a dialogue that takes place on a dramatic battlefield between Krishna and his devotee, Prince Arjuna. Its lesson is Karma Yoga, the mastery of being unattached to drama and action, of being free from fear, as we move towards liberation.

The Yoga Sutras

This brings us to the famous yoga era, where Patanjali reveals his Great Work. This happened during the Classical Epoch (AD 200–800), during which time the systemization of the philosophy made it easier to teach and share, and major schools of yoga started to flourish. The greatest work of this time was the Yoga Sutras of Patanjali, a written text that codified yoga and its philosophy. This work still teaches and offers clear guidelines to yoga students today.

Patanjali

According to the many interpretations of the Yoga Sutras, it is thought that Patanjali was a broad-minded man, a sage who accepted and explored all yogic teachings. His approach was more universal by nature. In teaching this

way, he made sure he showed respect to the many varied paths and religions, but chose not to teach from any one point of reference. Instead, he carefully chose his words and his concepts to be all accommodating and interfaith, instead of following one specific lineage. This could be why his teachings are still so profoundly appropriate to this modern age, although they were written so long ago.

Patanjali's 195 Truths

Patanjali's sutras see yoga as a systematic form or code that, once followed, will bring the student forward on their yogic path. The sutras share an overview of a given structure, a clear philosophy and discipline of yoga and meditation. The goals of this path are also made known in the sutras and can thereby be achieved if the system is closely followed. The goal of yoga is to be released from all obstructions, finding freedom from the wheel of life and achieving self-realization. The sutras were written in 195 short sayings that offered teachings of truth. Today, there are many translations and commentaries to help yoga students understand them more clearly.

Ashtanga Yoga

Patanjali's 195 definitions of truth outlining the basics of yoga are known as the Eight Limbs or Ashtanga. These Eight Limbs are also known as the threads that are worked though to bring about steps in progress. These threads are not linear, rather they are followed in an order according to the individual. Ashtanga Yoga contains eight systemized steps to follow, the ultimate goal being liberation.

Did You Know?

Patanjali's *The Yoga Sutras* – one of yoga's classic texts – is an ancient written document that helped to codify yoga and its philosophy. It is still read by yoga students around the world today.

The Eight Limbs

Patanjali's Eight Limbs, otherwise known as Ashtanga Yoga, are a sequential movement through a yogi's life journey. Each of the Eight Limbs are integrated and interrelated. They belong together, but can be stepped on and moved through in various orders. In a ladder-like formation, they move from gross and accessible to rarefied and spiritual. The path of yoga, following these steps, requires discipline and commitment if the goal is desired.

Yamas and Niyamas

At the base of the Eight-Limbed yogic path are the Yamas and Niyamas. A series of rules for right living, these cover the basic skills and values needed to prosper in the world, a kind of yoga code of conduct. In essence, the Yamas are the 'shall-not' rules and the Niyamas are the 'shall-do' rules.

Yamas
- Non-violence
- Absence of falsehood
- Non-stealing
- Sensory control/chastity
- Non-possessiveness

Niyamas
- Purity
- Contentment
- Determination
- Study
- Devotion

Asanas

These are postures for health and meditation, working with the physical body to strengthen and beautify. Working in this way, while being mindful of how you move, teaches the quality of grace. With asana practice, the student learns to train the inner body and the mind, which brings the intellect into sharper focus.

Pranayama

Prana is the life force that is in both the individual and the universe. Pranayama is the control of this life force, practising breathing exercises to bring about profound change in the physical body as well as lessening mind activity.

Pratyahara

Pranayama makes the mind fit to embrace Pratyahara. Pratyahara is the detachment from senses and thoughts, a natural progression from practising pranayama. When the mind manages detachment, senses withdraw and desires have less of an effect on the body. The mind turns within and freedom from attachment is achieved.

Dharana

Dharana is one-pointed concentration. This is the practice of focusing on one object or in one place to eliminate the mind's fluctuations. The focus can be external, such as on a candle, or it can be internal, such as on a part of the body or a mantra.

Dhyana

Progressing from Dharana, towards a more spiritual space, takes the individual to Dhyana, deep meditation. Here, the yogi has learned how to use the breath, how to detach and how to focus the mind. This is the time to cease all thought and, in the space of deep meditation, seek and realize the truth.

Samadhi

The final limb of Patanjali's teachings, Samadhi is the state of complete and integrated consciousness, in which the yogi is able to free himself from all that he is attached to and reach a place where he merges with the divine.

Checklist

☐ **Yoga is union:** Yoga is all about the union of the mind and body, to lift the student into higher levels of understanding and consciousness.

☐ **An ancient history:** The history of yoga can be traced back nearly 4,000 years, although it may date back even further, to prehistoric times.

☐ **Hatha Yoga:** Most forms of physical yoga in the West are some form of variation of traditional Hatha Yoga.

☐ **Six paths:** Hatha is one of the six yogic paths, which include following other, more spiritual and intellectual pursuits, as well as a physical practice.

☐ **The Yoga Sutras:** Patanjali was the first to document a written system of yoga technique and philosophy, in his Yoga Sutras.

☐ **Yamas and Niyamas:** These rules and guidelines for life give the yogi a code of conduct to follow, a list of what to do and what not to do.

☐ **Ashtanga Yoga:** Patanjali's Eight Limbs, otherwise known as Ashtanga Yoga – another popular yoga in the West – are a sequential movement through a yogi's life journey, like steps on a ladder.

☐ **The Holy Grail:** Samadhi is the final and ultimate goal, according to the Eight Limbs, where a yogi is set free and able to merge with the divine.

Getting Ready

Why Practise Yoga?

Yoga is the ultimate mind-body workout. Expect to see improved all-round wellness, greater energy levels and vitality. Expect weight loss, a firmer butt and tummy, and even a new-found twinkle in the eye. As well as giving a healthier body, yoga will strip away the mental clutter, as you breathe away everyday distractions. If you want to feel more relaxed, vibrant and alive, practise yoga.

Something for Everyone

Contrary to popular belief, you do not have to be bendy to take up yoga. That may well come in time, but the beauty of yoga is that it is suitable for all types, regardless of body shape, size or age. If you're just starting out, it's a fantastic way to limber up, and that's true even for the less bendy among us, or those with any limiting physical conditions. The great thing about yoga is that there really is something for everyone.

Just Do It

Here are 10 awesome reasons you should get stuck into yoga today:

✔ **Keeps you fit:** Yoga is a great exercise system for all-round body fitness.

✔ **Reduces stress:** Yoga is soothing, calming and contemplative.

- **Eases aches and pains**: Yoga can ease muscle tension and help with aches and pains.

- **Improves circulation**: Yoga stretching is great for getting you moving as nature intended.

- **Increases happiness**: Yoga helps to instill a sunnier disposition.

- **Boosts confidence**: Yoga can provide a strong mental uplift to boost confidence.

Did You Know?

The ultimate mind-body workout, yoga is not only great for losing weight and toning up your tummy, it's also the perfect stressbuster and confidence booster.

- **Helps you sleep more easily**: Yoga, and a restful body with rested muscles, can mean more and better sleep.

- **Is good for your sex life**: Research suggests that yoga can be a great way to raise your libido.

- **Helps you tone up**: Yoga is the perfect way to tone up and build your body beautiful.

- **Builds strength**: Yoga postures can also result in increased strength.

Just for You

Another beautiful thing about yoga is that there's no competitive aspect to it, so you can't lose. The only person you're competing with is yourself. When it comes down to it, it's just you and your mat, a chance to respect your body and what it can and cannot do. It's also a time to explore your inner mental and emotional state, to feel any stress or discomfort within you, and to respond accordingly. Yoga realigns body and mind, and teaches people how to understand what they're feeling, both physically and mentally. It's time just for you.

The Benefits of Yoga

The benefits of yoga are immense, hugely varied and, for many people, life-changing. Your own yoga practice will be as individual as you, and you can take from it precisely what you need. As well as the many physical effects, other benefits include an improvement in general wellbeing, increased confidence and greater inner calm. And for those that go on to pursue yoga further, it can lead to profound changes in how they view all areas of their life.

Getting Healthy

Taking up yoga is great for your body, and that's a fact. Even one hour-long class a week can make all the difference, especially for more mature students with fewer opportunities for physical activity or exercise. Some gentle exertion on the mat is an ideal way of staying active in later life, and indeed for all age groups. The health benefits of yoga are truly immense, and now very well documented among many scientific research papers.

Healthy on the Outside

Here are just some of the ways yoga will make you look and feel fabulous:

- **Improved flexibility:** Stretching exercises will inevitably give you more flexibility.

- **Greater strength:** Some weight-bearing yoga exercises will increase your strength.

- **Better balance:** Many postures require balance, a central theme of all yoga styles.

- **Improved muscle tone:** Regular yoga classes will also bring you improved muscle tone.

- **Increased stamina**: More-demanding yoga sessions will boost your stamina.

- **Weight loss**: Yoga can often bring weight-loss benefits, if desired.

- **Pain reduction**: Many students with pre-existing conditions have benefited from pain reduction after yoga.

- **Improved circulation**: Staying active on the mat will lead to improved circulation.

Healthy Mind

In today's hectic world, it's common for people to have very busy minds, making it hard to switch off. We're always thinking of work, what to do next, what bills we need to pay, so it's no wonder many people are suffering from stress and all the ill-effects that it can bring. The beauty of yoga is that it is an all-round mind-body workout. For the duration of your practice, your mind is enjoying some time out.

Healthy on the Inside

Here are some of the ways yoga will improve the inner you:

- **Stress relief**: Men and women commonly turn to yoga to help combat stress.

Top Tip

Chill out: take some extra time on the mat at the end of your class, or at home, to soak up some good peace vibes. Close your eyes and bliss out. This downtime is a super way to recharge your mental batteries.

- **Improved self-confidence**: Taking care of yourself through yoga can boost your self-confidence.

- **Enhanced mood**: Yoga will lift you up. Many people almost float out after class on a high.

- **Greater clarity**: It's easier to see things more clearly with a mind free from clutter.

- **More concentration**: Being relaxed in body and mind makes you sharper mentally.

- **Lessons in kindness and humility**: Yogis try to demonstrate kindness and respect where possible.

Lifestyle Benefits

As well as reprogramming your mind and firming up your body, yoga can lead to other, more subtle life changes. Spending time on the yoga mat offers moments of quiet reflection and contemplation, which can trigger deeper changes. This can be as simple as deciding to take better care of yourself by making healthier eating choices (many yogis choose to be vegetarian), or living a more simple, natural life.

Be the Change

Going forward, a greater awareness of your body and mind, and your all-round health, can often bring a more determined attitude to looking after yourself, and also projecting this out to the world. There is a famous quote by Gandhi about leading by example: 'Be the change that you wish to see in the world.' This is a motto adopted by many inspirational yogis who take on charitable projects or volunteer work to help those in need.

Who Can Do Yoga?

Anyone can do yoga, no matter their age, body shape or fitness level. The biggest challenge is always getting to class; the rest is easy. Yoga is not just for women either, with more and more men choosing to adopt a regular practice as part of a general health and wellbeing programme. Indeed, India's best-loved yoga founders and leaders have been male. Don't ever be nervous when entering a class: other people will have been just where you are.

Yoga for Seniors

Gentle, restorative yoga is a fabulous way for older people to maintain their flexibility and remain active. There are many classes and DVDs aimed specifically at mature yoga students. These may include gentler and more accessible postures, teaching proper spinal alignment at all times, with more attention given to pranayama (breathing exercises) or meditation.

Yoga for Babies And Children

Many parents enjoy taking their babies to yoga classes to allow them the freedom to stretch, relax and have fun in a safe setting. This offers physical stimulation for the baby and encourages co-ordination and flexibility, as well as promoting feelings of calm and relaxation. Yoga is great for younger children too, who enjoy the opportunity to stretch, play and grow, all in a fun and relaxing environment. Many of the positions in yoga have animal names (Downward Dog, Cat), which can be hugely appealing to children.

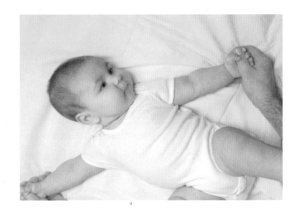

Yoga for Teens

Yoga is equally useful for older children, especially teenagers, as they navigate the pressures of this changing and turbulent time of life. While newcomers may be initially sceptical, a soothing yoga class offers a safe space for teenagers away from peer pressure, where they can soak up the relaxing vibes and de-stress. Yoga is ideal if they're facing exams or struggling with school or friendship issues.

Top Tip

Don't be shy. It's natural to be a bit nervous when you first enter a class, but your yoga teacher will have seen it all before. Tell them if you're a bit worried and they'll bend over backwards - possibly literally - to put you at ease.

Pre- and Post-Natal Yoga

Classes for new mums and mums-to-be abound. Yoga is the ideal way to allow the body space when it is going through such profound change. These classes are typically very gentle and adapted accordingly. For expectant mothers, yoga – and especially the breathing exercises –

is often a way of dealing with the pressure associated with giving birth. Breathing exercises can also be an invaluable aid during the birth. Equally, yoga is an excellent way for new mothers to gently return their bodies to their former glory.

Yoga for Men

For the most part, yoga is there for both men and women. However, some men accustomed to a gym environment might prefer a more active class, with little to no emphasis on the spiritual aspects of yoga. Some of yoga's weight-bearing postures are superb strength builders. There are very few male-only yoga classes, but some types of yoga (such as Hot Yoga, Bikram Yoga, or even Ashtanga) may seem more appealing for those seeking a more physical workout.

Be Careful

While yoga is there for everyone, that doesn't mean you can be reckless with your body. Those with medical conditions should always seek the advice of a qualified medical professional before commencing any new health and fitness programme. This is especially true if you are elderly or overweight or suffering from a known limiting physical condition or illness. In this case, your first port of call should always be your GP. A qualified yoga instructor will also be able to provide advice and reassurance where necessary.

Styles of Hatha Yoga

Although yoga can be very gentle, there are some more gruelling variations, so it's important to know what you're getting yourself into. Most common yoga styles are based around Hatha Yoga, but there can be quite a difference between the various styles.

Ashtanga Yoga

One of the stronger styles, this form of yoga was developed by K. Pattabhi Jois. Ashtanga practitioners move through a series of flows, from one posture to another, to build strength and to develop great flexibility and stamina. With a strong spiritual yoga message behind it, Ashtanga is not just an exercise class. It is not usually recommended for beginners or those seeking a more genteel approach to fitness.

Power Yoga

This is a fitness-based variant that derives from Ashtanga. Another physical and challenging yoga workout, the name Power Yoga means it can be popular and appealing to male yogis, or keep-fit fans, with its emphasis on strength and flexibility. It does not follow a set series of poses, unlike Ashtanga, which means classes can be very varied.

Vinyasa Yoga

This is a flowing style of yoga, where movement is synchronized with the breath (often called Vinyasa Flow). In this yoga, the poses run fluidly together, almost like a dance routine. The student moves in accordance with the breath, shifting from one pose to another on an inhale or an exhale. This close relationship between movement and breath is reflected in the Sanskrit translation of *vinyasa*, meaning 'connection'.

Iyengar Yoga

If ever there was a yoga done strictly by the book, then Iyengar is it. Developed by founder B.K.S. Iyengar, the emphasis here is on doing the asanas properly and correctly, even things as simple as standing up (Tadasana, or Mountain Pose). Iyengar is one of the most popular yoga styles in the world, where students pay extra close attention to detail to achieve precise alignment, using props such as blocks and belts if needed.

Satyananda Yoga

This form of yoga, developed by Sri Swami Satyananda Saraswati and his lineage, uses traditional asanas (postures), meditation and pranayama (breathing) to connect the physical body with the energy body. The approach encompasses the whole person, not just the body, with an open outlook to teaching and encouraging the yoga lifestyle.

Did You Know?

Yoga comes in all shapes and sizes, but most forms that you're likely to come across in the local studio are variations of Hatha Yoga.

Kundalini Yoga

Kundalini, an amalgam of yoga involving classic asanas, breath work, mantra and meditation, was brought to the West by Yogi Bhajan. It focuses on building physical, mental and spiritual strength, where you uncoil yourself and your energy within to find your potential and vitality in order to reach your virtues. It is sometimes called the Yoga of Awareness.

Viniyoga

This form of yoga is highly individualized, where a teacher works closely with a single student, to create a personalized programme based on key life factors such as age, health and physical condition. Yoga postures and routines may be adapted to take into account all of these factors. It is the opposite of a one-size-fits-all approach, common in many basic Hatha classes.

Bikram Yoga

Founded by Bikram Choudhury, this is where you get hot and sweaty, performing 26 asanas in sequence in a heated studio. It's very physical and gruelling and generally not something recommended for total novices, but great if you're an athlete. The idea is that your body is far less prone to injury in the heated environment. There are many non-Bikram linked, Hot Yoga centres around offering a similar thing.

Sivananda Yoga

Another hugely popular style, Sivananda also follows a structure that includes the use of pranayama, classic asanas and relaxation. However, unlike some of the more dynamic yoga styles, it revolves around frequent relaxation, including full, yogic breathing. This form of yoga follows the teachings of Swami Sivananda, and was brought to the West by one of his disciples, Swami Vishnudevananda.

Finding A Class

If you're a total novice, the best place to start yoga is at a class, with a qualified instructor and some other students to keep you company and motivate you. This is especially true if you have any medical conditions. For any new exercise regime, it's always best to seek medical advice, although your yoga teacher should also be able to advise you.

Spoilt for Choice

There are new yoga studios and classes popping up all over the country. In the big cities, you can take your pick, with a huge range of options offering every type of yoga imaginable. If you live in a rural location, however, your options may be limited. Be realistic about what you can and can't do. There's no point signing up for classes in a shiny new city-centre yoga studio that looks fantastic but will be a real pain to get to. But if you can fit in the class after work before you head home, no problem.

Suits You

Be sure to pick a class that's pitched at your level of ability. Generally speaking, yoga classes of all types are flagged up as suitable either for beginners, intermediates or advanced levels. If you're really out of shape, you'd be wise to avoid one of the more strenuous yoga styles. If you're not sure about something, just ask. The vast majority of yoga teachers are very approachable and will do all they can to make you feel at ease in their class.

What Do You Want?

If you're after a demanding physical workout, Hot Yoga or Bikram Yoga may suit you well. If you want a quieter and more meditative practice, Sivananda might be better. For most people, any beginner's Hatha class is a good entry point, offering an introduction to the postures, coupled with a spot of calm relaxation or meditation afterwards.

Top Tip

Remember: be realistic when choosing a class. The most important thing is to actually make your yoga session each week, so, however flashy the studio, there's no point signing up if it's a struggle for you to get to each time.

Where to Look

Yoga classes are everywhere – you just need to know where to look. Here are some suggestions:

- **Ask around:** Ask friends if they know a yoga teacher; personal recommendation is always best.

- **Local newspapers:** Check the listings inside local newspapers for classes near you.

- **Visit the library:** Local libraries are a gold mine for all types of community information.

- **Notice boards:** Many shops and supermarkets have local community notice boards.

- **Search the web:** Search for local yoga studios on the internet and see what comes up.

- **Buy a magazine:** Buy a specialist yoga magazine to research some of the different yoga styles out there, and thus which classes might be best for you.

The Art of Self-Practice

Once you've picked up a few basics in class, you might want to start trying some simple yoga moves at home. This is a good way to step up your yoga practice, learn your own way, and in your own time. Later on, you can expand this to other locations, when you're on holiday, for example, or even at work. You can take your yoga wherever you go.

The Home Front

As well as the obvious benefits (it's free and you can do it in the comfort of your own home), developing a self-practice is the next logical step in your yoga journey. For the more dedicated, yoga is not something that can be confined to a one-hour class, but it is a lifelong experience, traversing all aspects of life. However, a home practice doesn't mean you give up your classes; it's great to keep up with your yoga buddies by attending sessions with an instructor to keep you motivated and on track.

How to Start a Home Practice

If you can allocate a dedicated spot in your home for yoga, that's ideal. This is a place where you have room to roll out your mat and stretch out when time permits. If you really want to go for it, start making that space beautiful, surrounding yourself with sumptuous smells, soothing sounds and soft lighting. It's not essential, but it makes the experience so much more therapeutic. Try to allocate a small block of time each day, and stick with it. However, juggling a busy life may make this tricky, so be flexible and do not beat yourself up if you slip up; just start again the next day. Little and often is the key.

Everyday Yoga

If you can incorporate yoga into your everyday life, this is where you really feel the benefits of self-practice. Look for opportunities throughout your day to enjoy some gentle restorative poses, or a spot of quiet relaxation, in your lunch hour, or when you're waiting in the car to pick the kids up from school. Here are some other ideas:

- **At work:** If you sit at a desk all day long, stretch your back and neck out as much as possible. Take regular walking breaks, even if just to the toilet.

- **In the car:** Try not to fret when you're stuck in traffic; yoga helps us to manage stressful situations, so use the opportunity to calmly control your thoughts and emotions.

- **Waiting for the bus:** Don't just stand, stand proud. Practise Mountain Pose (Tadasana) and stand up tall, straight and confident.

- **In the supermarket:** If you're in a long checkout queue, don't huff and puff. Try using yoga breathing techniques to instill a greater sense of calm.

Top Tip

You know you've arrived when you start to throw some yoga moves into your everyday routine. Look for opportunities to stretch your legs and arms, back and neck wherever you go: in the car, in the shopping line, or at your desk.

Yoga Essentials

The beauty of yoga is you don't really need anything to do it. Not even a mat. Having said that, a whole industry has developed to cater to the modern yogi's every whim, from super-cool designer clothing to eco-friendly water bottles that will last a lifetime.

What to Wear

Clothing should be loose fitting and practical to allow your body the freedom to move. Think tracksuit bottoms, shorts, or lycra if you're bold enough.

Yoga Kit

Here are some of the main things you can buy if you want your own yoga kit:

- **Clothing:** There is a huge range of yoga kit on the market.

- **Socks:** For hygiene reasons, some people like to wear socks, though these aren't practical in every posture. Toe socks – socks with individual toes, like gloves – are popular, as they provide a little extra grip.

Top Tip

When you're just starting out, save your money. You don't need to buy anything at first, not even a mat. As your keenness builds, that's when you can start to explore the big wide world of yoga clothing and accessories.

Props: Blocks, bolsters and ties can be useful to assist and enhance your postures.

DVDs: These are great if you want to start or develop your yoga practice at home.

Music: Some gentle music is great for your home practice and for meditation.

Mats

In ancient India, yogis would simply go barefoot. That still goes on: many in the West still enjoy going barefoot in the park. But in virtually every organized class, students practise on mats. Consequently, mats are nearly always supplied, or available to hire, in class, but check with your teacher. As you progress, or your interest deepens (or if you just want a mat that hasn't been trodden on by others' sweaty feet), then it makes sense to get your own mat. If you decide to buy your own, there is a dizzying choice. Some have extra cushioning; some are smaller, some are bigger; some are lightweight and ideal for travel. Many mats have strong environmentally friendly credentials.

There are even crystal-encrusted mats for the full Hollywood experience, with a price tag to match. Choose according to your budget and understand what your requirements are; though it is probably best to go for a cheap, basic mat at first – you can always upgrade later.

Above: Mat bags and carry-all bags can be useful to the yoga devotee

The Yoga Diet

Yoga's focus on the body naturally leads to a greater awareness of what is good (and what is bad) for you. Healthy eating choices are an integral part of a committed yoga practice. There is no real focus on dieting or weight loss in yoga, rather on food choices that complement the body and support optimum health.

Life Force

Everything that we eat and drink, even the air that we breathe, contains amounts of life-force energy (or prana), which is essential for our wellbeing and longevity. All food has this quality, but natural, raw and unprocessed foods are clearly more wholesome, delivering more prana than refined and processed products such as ready meals made in factories and bought in packages ready for microwave heating.

The Sattvic Diet

Foods are sometimes classified into three groups (Sattvic, Tamasic and Rajasic), with each delivering higher or lower amounts of energy, and affecting the body in different ways. The healthy yoga choice is a diet rich in Sattvic foods (predominantly natural fruits and vegetables), though many Western households now sway more to Tamasic foods (meat and processed products).

 Sattvic: Fresh, juicy, light, nourishing, sweet and tasty foods (such as juicy fruits and vegetables, fresh milk and butter, grains and nuts). These easily digested foods provide a large amount of energy to the body without taxing it.

- **Tamasic:** Dry, old or decaying foods, or foods that have been heavily processed (such as meat, fish and eggs). These foods take a large amount of energy from the body while being digested.

- **Rajasic:** These are bitter and sour, or salty and pungent, and can be hot and dry (such as foods fried in oil, or cooked too much). These foods can speed up the human organism – in other words, they are overstimulating, can make the mind more agitated.

Top Tip

If you haven't made it to class, don't worry: yoga is about looking after your whole self and that includes what you put into it. So take some time and prepare a healthy and nutritious meal in the evening for you and your loved ones instead.

The Right Stuff

While Sattvic foods may be the healthiest choice, it is not always possible (or advisable) to leap into a complete dietary change. However, achieving a more balanced diet as part of a yoga practice is both possible and relatively easy. As a general rule, avoid processed foods, especially sugar, and other additives and opt for natural produce. The cornerstones of any healthy yoga diet are always fresh fruits and vegetables. And to know what you are eating, food is best prepared at home in your kitchen.

Checklist

☐ **Inside out:** Yoga can make you feel fabulous inside and out. The total mind and body workout, yoga will tone you up and calm you down.

☐ **Never too old:** Yoga is for everyone. You are never too old, too overweight, too inflexible to take up yoga.

☐ **Know your styles:** It's fun to experiment with yoga styles, so visit a new class whenever you can to mix things up a bit.

☐ **Born free:** You don't need any gear or kit to start yoga, just get to that first class and do it.

☐ **Portable yoga:** Yoga can be done anywhere and at any time. Learn a few postures and breathing exercises, then take them wherever you go.

☐ **Home space:** Allocate a small area of your home as your own private yoga studio. Light some candles, play some soothing music and away you go.

☐ **Healthy eating:** Start including more fruits and vegetables into your diet, and cut down on processed foods.

☐ **In the kitchen:** If you cook with raw ingredients at home, then you know exactly where your food has come from. No nasty surprises from processed factory foods.

The Postures

The Asanas

Now you've read about the benefits and beginnings of yoga, it's time to put your knowledge into practice. Remember to begin slowly and carefully, and if something hurts, stop immediately. It's unlikely you'll be able to do all the postures straightaway, as some are more advanced and require time, practice and patience.

Begin Gradually

The following postures have been organized to help you ease into your yoga practice, beginning with standing postures, before leading on to sitting postures and finally floor-based postures. By following the rhythm of the next few pages, your body will gradually and fully warm up, so that by the time you try a Shoulderstand you'll be physically and emotionally ready to attempt it.

Begin Calmly

Yoga is about more than movement. It's also about calming the brain, opening the heart and allowing any resistance to disappear. You may find that when you begin your yoga practice, you're stiff, your mind may be whirring, and you'll probably just want the routine to end! As you practise more and more, and start to welcome the opportunity to rest your mind and stretch your body (even if it's not very much at first), your body will follow the example set by your mind, and open and relax.

Do What's Right For You

Remember, never force a movement. If a posture hurts in any way, stop immediately. A good idea is to return to Child Pose (page 89) to rest your body and calm your mind, before attempting the posture again. And always reverse your steps slowly to return ro neutral. Build up your stretches over time to ensure you don't overdo it or cause injury. If you can only reach your knees when you're stretching out in front, then accept that as today's achievement. Within a few weeks of regular practice, you'll find that your body becomes more flexible and the poses become more natural.

There's no right or wrong number of poses to do. If all you achieve each morning is a Sun Salutation (page 196), then that's still an achievement. Over time, your routine will come naturally and develop organically. Above all, remember to breathe.

Now let's get started.

What You'll Need

- ✍ **Loose, comfortable clothing**
- ✍ **A yoga mat or double-folded towel**
- ✍ **A blanket (to support your head and for warmth before and after your routine)**
- ✍ **A block**
- ✍ **A bolster**
- ✍ **Stretchy bands or a yoga belt**

Standing Postures

Standing postures are the basis of yoga. All standing poses have one thing in common: they'll improve your posture, balance and overall strength. Keep both feet planted firmly on the ground, with your toes spread evenly on your mat. This sounds easier than it really is, as most of us naturally lean towards one side. This natural lean can cause back and hip pain and even headaches. By learning how to readjust your balance, you'll improve your ability to concentrate, and prevent or mitigate back problems.

What They Do

Standing poses strengthen the leg muscles and joints, and increase the suppleness and strength of the spine. Due to their rotational and flexing movements, the spinal muscles and intervertebral joints are kept mobile and well aligned. The arteries of the legs are stretched, increasing the blood supply to the lower limbs, preventing thrombosis in the calf muscles. These poses also tone the cardiovascular system, increasing the supply of blood to the heart.

Stand to Gain

A result of correcting your balance in standing postures is long, lean and strengthened legs. Good posture, which is achieved through regular yoga practice, means that your legs, pelvis, hips and groin all

become strengthened. A 2010 study published in the *European Journal of Physical and Rehabilitation Medicine* found that yoga can be an effective treatment for those with osteoporosis, a condition which affects more than 200 million people worldwide.

Most importantly, the standing poses ensure that you're 'grounded' and present for your session. Becoming aware of the way you stand is one of the first steps to correcting your posture, not just during a yoga session, but at all times throughout the day. By standing tall, with legs strong, abdominal muscles and buttocks firm, hips and chest area open, you're engaging your entire body.

Mountain Pose (Tadasana)

Tadasana implies a pose where one stands firm and erect as a mountain. Practising it gives rise to a sense of firmness, strength, stillness and steadiness. It's a relaxed, welcoming position, which can help to improve your posture and balance. It can also be a great pose for slowing and modulating your breathing.

1 **Stand** tall but relaxed with your feet together, or slightly apart if this places strain on your back. Your second toes should be parallel to each other.

2 **Palms towards your thighs**, arms hanging gently at your sides.

3 **Feel the floor** under your feet, and spread your weight evenly across your feet, heels and toes. Slowly rock side to side and back and forth – this will help you find your centre.

4 **Bend your knees slightly**. This should take pressure away from your lower back.

5 **Straighten your legs slowly**, bringing the knees directly over the ankles and the hips directly over the knees.

Without using your stomach muscles, activate your thigh muscles and lift your kneecaps.

6 **Turn the upper thighs** very slightly inwards, without moving your hips.

Top Tip

Mountain Pose is the starting point for all standing poses, but it's a good idea to practise this pose on its own. It will help to relieve sciatica, improve your posture and strengthen your thighs, knees, ankles, abdomen and glutes.

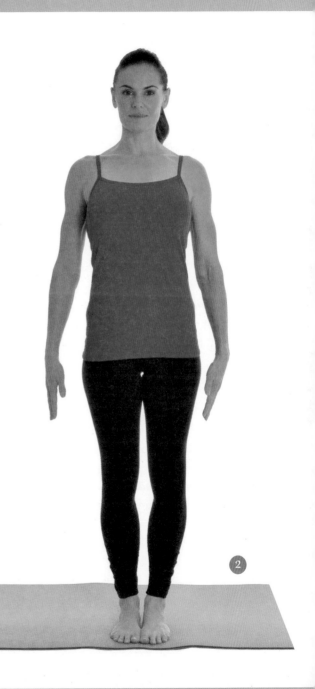

7 **Gently pull** your shoulder blades back, down your back, without tensing your neck muscles.

8 **Lift your sternum** (your chest) towards the ceiling. Keep your upper body steady and don't be tempted to push your ribs forwards.

9 **Keep the stomach in**, chest forward, spine stretched up and the neck straight.

10 **Flare your collarbones**, making sure your shoulders are parallel to your pelvis.

11 **Keep your facial muscles soft**, your chin parallel to the floor, and your tongue relaxed against the floor of your mouth.

12 **Stay in this pose** for around 30 seconds to one minute, keeping your breath soft and slow.

Top Tip

If you're pregnant, keep your feet hip-distance apart.

Tree Pose (Vrksasana)

A great pose to perfect your balance and poise. It may help your balance to focus on a spot a metre or so in front of you. Your thighs and calves will benefit enormously from this posture.

1. **Begin in Mountain Pose** (page 58), breathe slowly and evenly for 10 seconds.

2. **Slowly shift your weight** to the left foot, while keeping the left foot firmly planted on the floor.

Top Tip

This pose helps to improve your bone density, so it's a great posture for women, particularly for those approaching, or going through, the menopause. This is also a great posture to ground and centre the body, giving rise to emotional and mental balance. It opens the hips, tones the legs and improves balance.

2

3. **Bend your right knee** and slowly, looking straight ahead, reach down with your right hand and clasp your right ankle. If you can't reach that far, take hold of your right calf.

4. **Bring the right foot up** and place the sole against the inside left thigh. Take it as high as you can – to the left groin if possible. If this is difficult, gently place the sole of the right foot against your

left calf. Your toes should point towards the floor. Lift your arms above your head.

5. **Check your posture** to ensure your pelvis hasn't shifted to the left. If you need to, readjust your balance, keeping your pelvis centred.

6. **Press your right foot** more firmly against the inner left thigh and strengthen your left thigh by resisting the pressure. This will help to lengthen your tailbone towards the floor and stretch your lower back muscles.

7. **Bring your hands** gently together. Fix your attention on a spot on the floor around one metre in front of you and relax your gaze.

8. **Hold** this position for around 30 seconds to one minute.

9. **Return to Mountain Pose** on an exhaled breath. Repeat on the opposite side.

7

Caution

Take care if you have unstable sacroiliac joints, low or high blood pressure. If you have high blood pressure, don't take your arms above your head; if you have low blood pressure, don't stay in the pose for too long.

Chair Pose (Utkatasana)

For such an innocuous-sounding posture, the Chair Pose packs a powerful punch. Try it and see how fierce and strong you feel afterwards. As the name suggests, this asana is like sitting in an imaginary chair.

1. **Begin in Mountain Pose** (page 58). Breathe slowly and deeply. Breathe in, lifting your arms straight over your head towards the ceiling, palms facing towards each other. Keep your sternum lifted and draw your shoulder blades down your back, away from your ears.

2. **Exhale**, bend your knees, so that your thighs are almost parallel to the floor. Your knees will be slightly further forward than your toes, and your upper body will lean forwards, over your thighs. Continue stretching forwards, with your arms stretched up over your head, until your torso is as close to a right angle with your thighs as possible. Your spine should be straight from the top of your head to your tailbone.

3. **Keep your inner thighs** pressed firmly against each other. Check that

3

you are pressing into both feet and not leaning to one side. Check that your shoulders haven't risen upwards – keep your shoulder blades pulled down and your bottom tucked under.

4. **Hold** this position for 30 seconds to one minute.

5. **Return to Mountain Pose** by firstly straightening your knees, and using your arms as momentum, bringing them above your head. Once standing, breathe out and return your arms to your sides.

Top Tip

This pose strengthens the legs and ankles. The diaphragm is lifted and this gives a gentle massage to the heart. If you have problems with your lower back or stomach muscles, perform this pose near a wall. Stand around eight centimetres away from it, so that, when you are in position, your tailbone gently touches, and is supported by, the wall.

Triangle Pose (Trikonasana)

This pose is ideal for those who are pregnant, suffering from PMT aches and pains, or feeling the stresses and strains after a difficult day. It strengthens and tones the legs and ankles. It also gives a gentle lateral extension which strengthens the side and back body.

1. **Stand in Mountain Pose** (page 58). Breathe out and step, or lightly jump, your feet shoulder-width apart.

2. **Slowly raise your arms** outwards in line with your shoulders, so that a straight line runs from one palm to the other, parallel to the floor. Keep your shoulder blades open and wide, neck relaxed and palms facing downwards.

Top Tip

Going into a stressful meeting? Perform this pose once on either side to help relieve feelings of anxiety.

3. **Turn your left foot** slightly towards your right (around 15 degrees) and turn your right foot out (90 degrees). Both heels should be aligned. Make your thighs strong by drawing your kneecaps up. Turn your right thigh towards the right foot, until the centre of the right kneecap is directly above the centre of the right foot. It is important for the knee not to move. It should stay aligned with the second toe at all times. Keep your quadriceps drawn up.

4. **On an out breath**, bend the trunk sideways to the right, over the right leg.

Keep the kneecaps drawn up. Bend from your hips, not your waist, ensuring that your pelvis stays static. Your back should be flat. (Imagine being like a slice of bread going into a toaster, or practise with your back up against a wall). The back of the legs, the back of the chest and the hips should all be in one line. Bring the right palm near the right ankle. Stretch the left arm up, bringing it in line with the right shoulder and extend the trunk. Ensure that your tailbone and the back of your head align with each other.

5. **Rest your hand** where you can (the shin, ankle or floor) outside the right foot. Make sure your upper body hasn't shifted, and that the whole body is in one plane. (If you have neck problems, keep your head in neutral and don't look up – look straight ahead.)

6. **Hold** this pose for 30 seconds to one minute.

7. **Inhale** to return to the starting position, keeping both arms extended. Use your heels, not your stomach muscles or lower back, to perform this move. Repeat on the left side.

Half-Moon Pose (Ardha Chandrasana)

This asana is an ideal pose to help balance out your left and right sides. It looks difficult, but, as it helps to build thigh strength, it's a great toning posture and is a natural progression from Triangle Pose.

1. **Repeat the steps for Triangle Pose** (page 65). Once you have placed your right hand onto your shin, ankle or to the right of your foot, rest your left hand on your left hip.

2. **Take a deep breath**, and slowly and gently slide your left foot 15 to 30 centimetres forwards. Simultaneously, reach forwards with your right hand, around 30 centimetres away from your little toe on your right foot.

3. **Breathe out**, firmly grounding your right hand and right heel. Straighten your right leg and lift your left leg until it's as close to

Top Tip

Keep looking straight ahead if you have any neck problems, don't turn your head to look upwards. Avoid this pose if you are tired, suffer from stress-related headaches, migraines, eyestrain, varicose veins, diarrhoea or insomnia.

parallel to the floor as possible. Feel the stretch all the way through to your left heel, without locking your left knee. Your right leg should be strong, but not overextended.

4. **Keep your left arm** stretched up, in line with your right arm, opening your collarbones.

5. **Keep your hips** facing forwards and rotate your upper body towards the ceiling. Keep your head in a neutral position looking straight ahead, unless you are more advanced and can begin to look up towards the ceiling.

6. **With your bodyweight** on your right foot, thigh and hip, use your right hand to balance yourself and adjust your hip position if necessary. Continue to feel the stretch from the tip of your head, through your shoulder blades, lower back, thighs, groin, calf and ankle.

7. **Hold** this position for as long as feels comfortable – around 30 seconds to one minute. Lower the left leg on an out breath and return to Triangle Pose. Repeat on the opposite side.

5

Warrior Pose 1 (Virabhadrasana)

This is a great posture to ground and centre the body, giving rise to emotional and mental balancing. It opens the hips, tones the legs and ankles and improves balance. This is one of two Warrior Poses we show. Begin with this pose and work your way up to the more difficult version.

1. **Stand in Mountain Pose** (page 58). Breathe in and, on the out breath, step or jump to place your feet around one metre apart.

2. **Raise your arms** so that they're over your head, parallel to each other, and perpendicular to the floor. Concentrate on stretching fully through the little fingers on each hand, reaching towards the ceiling.

3. **Continue stretching upwards**, and concentrate on pulling your shoulder blades back and down your back.

4. **Turn your left foot** 45 to 60 degrees to the right and the right foot 90 degrees to the right. Make sure that your heels are in line.

Top Tip

It's easy to overdo this stretch, which can result in a strained lower back. Make sure that your pelvis is tipped forwards, towards your navel, whilst simultaneously lengthening your coccyx towards the floor.

5. **Inhale** and, as you exhale, turn your torso to the right, keeping your pelvis centred. Your left hip should be pointing forwards. Don't be tempted to lift your left foot – instead, concentrate on keeping it firmly planted on the mat.

6. **As you lean forward**, your lower back should naturally elongate towards the floor – your chest and upper body will lean slightly backwards.

7. **As you breathe out**, bend your right knee over the right ankle. Make sure that your shin is perpendicular to the floor, and that your knee isn't hanging over your right foot.

8. **Lift upwards** through your arms, towards the ceiling. If you can, place your palms together, pressing firmly through the little fingers on each hand.

9. **Keep your head still** if you suffer from neck problems; otherwise look up through your hands.

10. **Hold** this pose for 30 seconds to a minute. Return to the starting position by reversing the above steps: straighten your right knee, turn your feet to point forwards, and lower your arms on an out breath.

11. **Repeat** the steps above on the opposite side.

12. **When you've performed the pose on each side**, return to Mountain Pose.

8

Warrior Pose II (Virabhadrasana)

This is a more advanced version of the Warrior Pose I. Move on to this posture when you've become comfortable with the easier version.

1. **Stand in Mountain Pose** (page 58). Breathe out and jump your feet one metre apart.

2. **Raise your arms** so that they're parallel to the floor, palms facing down.

3. **Turn your right foot** slightly to the right, and your left foot out through 90 degrees to the left. Both heels should be in one line. Make

your thighs strong, and turn your left thigh outwards, until the centre of the left kneecap is in line with your left heel.

4. **Exhale** and bend your left knee until it's slightly over the left ankle. Your shin should be perpendicular to the floor. Continue stretching (if you can) until your left thigh is parallel to the floor.

Top Tip

If you cannot execute the full stretch, try bending your knee less. If you cannot maintain the stretch and balance well at the same time, you may also find it easier to keep your hands on your hips.

5. **Continue** to press the outer right heel onto the mat.

6. **Continue** to lift and stretch your arms outwards. Your shoulder blades should be relaxed, but open down your back.

7. **Look to your left** over your fingertips. Hold this position for 30 seconds, working your way up to one minute. Inhale to return to standing position. Repeat on the opposite side.

6

Extended-Angle Pose (Parsavakonasana)

This is a lovely posture to open your ribs, hips and inner thighs. It enhances lung capacity, tones the heart, improves digestion and helps the elimination of waste. This pose also relieves sciatic and arthritic pains.

1. **Begin in Mountain Pose** (page 58). Breathing out, step or lightly jump your feet around one metre, or shoulder-width, apart.

2. **Raise your arms** parallel to the floor, without lifting or tensing your neck. Keep your palms facing downwards, and your shoulder blades open and relaxed. You may need to attempt this a couple of times before your neck and shoulders feel loose.

3. **Turn your left foot in** slightly to the right, and turn your right foot to the right at a 90-degree angle to the direction you're facing. Both heels should be in one line.

4. **Draw your thighs upwards**, and turn your right thigh out (you can use your hands to turn it if need be). Your right kneecap should be in line with your heel.

5. **Slowly shift your left hip** forwards, towards the right, taking care to keep your upper chest and torso focused to the left.

6. **Ground your left heel**, ensuring the entire foot is touching the mat evenly. Breathe out, and bend your right knee over the right ankle to a 90-degree angle. Bend as far as you can, ideally until your right thigh is parallel to the floor.

6

7. **Extend your left arm** towards the ceiling, and turn the left palm to face inwards, towards your ear. Breathe out, and stretch up and over your head, keeping your arm close to your left ear. You should feel a stretch from your left heel all the way to the tips of your fingers on your left hand. Use both legs evenly, taking care not to put all your weight onto the right leg.

8. **If you feel comfortable** doing so, turn your head to look up at your left arm, without twisting your body. As you continue to stretch, extend further on the out breath and, if you can, lay the right side of your body as close as possible to the top of the right thigh.

9. **Bend right** towards the floor with your fingers (or palm if you can), and press downwards slightly to the right of your right foot. Use a block if this helps.

10. **Push with your right knee** against the inner arm, without hunching over. Ensure that your pelvis is still centred.

11. **Hold** this position for 30 seconds to one minute. As you inhale, return to the starting position. Repeat on the other side and return to the starting pose.

9

Wide-Legged Forward Bend
(Prasarita Padottanasana)

This is a wonderful stretching exercise for your lower torso and upper thighs. It also helps to still a busy, anxious mind, cooling the body and brain and giving you a feeling of tranquillity and repose.

1. **Stand in Mountain Pose** (page 58), so that you're facing the longer side of the mat. Place your feet shoulder-width apart.

2. **Gently rest your hands** on your hips, and check that your feet are facing forwards, parallel to each other. Make sure your weight is spread evenly across your feet. This will help to make your thighs 'strong', by drawing up the thigh muscles. Step your feet about one metre apart, keeping your feet parallel.

3. **Breathe in**, and slightly lift your chest, so that the front of your body is longer than the back.

4. **Hold** this stretch and lean forwards, from the hips, until your upper body is parallel to the floor. Reach downwards, and press your fingertips onto

2

the floor, directly below your shoulders. Your arms should be parallel, your back slightly curved, and your stomach pulled in towards your spine.

5. **Slightly raise** your head, so that your eyes are looking towards the ceiling.

6. **Check your thighs**, and strengthen them by pushing your thighs backwards. You should feel this in your groin, hips and lower back, but don't push too hard if you feel pain. Relax here for a moment, breathing deeply and evenly. Try to keep your sitting bones tilted

up towards the ceiling. Pull in your tailbone, work both legs and feet evenly, remembering to push the ball of the big toe into the floor.

7. **Slowly walk your fingertips** between your feet, towards your groin. Maintain this position and continue to take slow, deep breaths. On the out breath, bend your elbows and, leaning forward, lower your upper body and head towards the floor, resting your palms on the floor between your thighs. For those who are flexible, you may be able to rest the top of your head on the floor.

8. **Continue to press your palms** into the floor, keeping your fingers pointing forwards.

9. **ADVANCED MOVE**: Continue to bend forwards until your forearms are resting on the floor. Your arms should be evenly placed next to each other and your shoulder blades open wide across your back.

10. **Hold** this pose for 30 seconds to one minute. To return to the starting position, lift your arms, so that your hands are now on the floor, and lift and lengthen your front torso forwards. Breathe in and rest your hands on your hips, slightly tucking your tailbone under to bring your torso upwards. Walk or lightly jump into Mountain Pose position.

Caution

If you're a beginner, do not hold this pose for more than one minute. If you have low blood pressure, come out of the pose gradually to avoid dizziness.

Standing Forward Bend (Uttanasana)

If you suffer from headaches, or constantly feel run down, depressed or tired, try starting and ending your day with this posture. It'll perk you up – like an all-over massage.

1. **Begin in Mountain Pose** (page 58), with your feet hip-width apart and your hands on your hips, breathing slowly.

2. **Exhale** and bend forwards from the hips, imagining that your upper body is stretching out of your groin, and opening the area between the pubis and sternum. Keep the arches of your feet lifted by pressing the ball of the big toe into the floor. This will lift your inner ankles and increase the lift of the quadriceps.

3. **Keeping your knees straight** and strong, place your fingertips or, if you can, your palms slightly in front of or beside your feet. If you can reach the backs of your ankles,

Top Tip

Perform this pose when resting between the standing poses to rejuvenate and relax your body. Avoid this pose if you have bulging discs. If your hamstrings are tight, you can slightly bend the knees.

gently grasp them. For those beginning and not able to reach the floor, cross your forearms and hold your elbows or use blocks for your hands to rest on. Your heels should be firmly grounded, thighs turned sightly inwards and your bottom facing the ceiling.

4. **Inhale**, lift and lengthen the front of your upper body. With each exhalation, stretch a little further forward. Keep your neck soft, eyes downwards.

5. **Return** to standing by using your tailbone and pelvis, not your hips. Keep your upper body stretched forwards, breathing out as you do so.

4

Single-Leg Forward Bend (Parsvottanasana)

This is a difficult-looking pose, which is an intense stretch to the sides of the chest and hamstrings. Because it is a forward bend, it is very calming for the body and soul.

1. **Stand with feet together**, your hands gently resting on your hips.

2. **Lift your left foot** and place it around 60 centimetres in front. It should be in line with your left hip.

3. **Exhale**, keeping the legs straight, and bend at the hips so that your torso comes forwards over the left leg. Keep the spine as straight as possible, your head facing downwards towards your left leg, neck loose.

4. **Reach downwards** with both arms, placing your fingertips on the floor, either side of the left foot. Make sure your shoulders don't rise up. Keep your shoulder blades down and wide across your back. If you can't touch the floor, use blocks under your hands. Keep your kneecaps drawn up and hips evenly facing forward. Try to keep your sternum lifted so the front body is kept long rather than collapsed.

5. **Hold** for 30 seconds, breathing slowly and evenly. Return your hands to your hips and slowly raise your upper body and return to starting position. Repeat on the opposite side.

Top Tip

If you can stretch further, place your palms on the floor, and rest your forehead on your left shin.

Eagle Pose (Garudasana)

This asana develops the ankles, helps with leg cramps and removes stiffness to the shoulders. When you perform this pose, you'll see why Garudasana is translated as 'eagle pose', although its literal meaning comes from to 'devour'. Feel the power rise as you perfect this posture.

1. **Begin in Mountain Pose** (page 58). Bend your knees slightly, lift your right foot up and, balancing on your left foot, cross your right thigh over the left one. Point your right toes downwards, then hook the top of the right foot behind the lower left calf.

2. **Balance** on your left foot, distributing your weight evenly and firmly over it. Focus on a point around one metre in front of you to help keep your balance.

3. **Stretch your arms forwards**, keeping them parallel to the floor and level with your shoulders. Cross your arms in front of your torso so that the left arm is above the right, then bend your elbows. Tuck the left elbow into the crook of the right, and raise your forearms perpendicular to the floor. The backs of your hands should be facing each other.

4. **Press** the left hand to the left and the right hand to the right so that the palms are now facing each other. The thumb of the right hand should pass in front of the little finger of the left. Now press the palms together (as much as is possible for you), lift your elbows up, and stretch your fingers towards the ceiling.

5. **Hold** for 15 to 30 seconds, then unwind your legs and arms and return to Mountain Pose. Repeat for the same length of time with the arms and legs reversed.

Dancer's Pose (Natarajasana)

This difficult pose develops poise and a graceful carriage. It tones and strengthens the leg muscles. The shoulder blades get full movement and the chest expands fully.

1. **Stand in Mountain Pose** (page 58). Stretch the right arm out in front, keeping it parallel to the floor. Bend the left knee and lift up the left foot. Hold the left big toe between the thumb and the index and middle fingers of the left hand. Bend the lifted left knee and draw the leg up and back.

2. **Roll the fingers and thumb** of the left hand around the left big toe. Simultaneously rotate the left elbow and shoulder and stretch the left arm up behind the head, without releasing the grip on the big toe. Again, pull the left arm and leg up so that they form a bow behind your back.

1

3. **Bring the right arm straight in front**, level with the shoulder, keeping the fingers pointing forward.

4. **Pull the kneecap up** and keep the right leg poker stiff and perpendicular to the floor. Balance firmly from 10 to 15 seconds, with deep and even breathing.

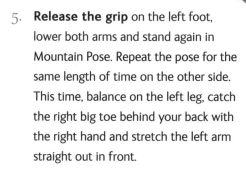

5. **Release the grip** on the left foot, lower both arms and stand again in Mountain Pose. Repeat the pose for the same length of time on the other side. This time, balance on the left leg, catch the right big toe behind your back with the right hand and stretch the left arm straight out in front.

6. **ADVANCED MOVE**: Hold the foot with both hands, rest it on the head and balance.

4

Sitting and Floor Postures

Did you know that we sit for around 15 hours every day? That's 90 per cent of our waking time! Which means these sitting poses should be simple, right? Think again. Sitting at a desk, or in front of the television, for hours every day shortens your hamstrings, and if you have poor posture, can reduce the effectiveness of your core strength.

Stretch and Bend for Health

Mastering seated poses will help to stretch out those hamstrings and tendons, reduce lower back pain and strengthen your abdominal muscles. Most importantly, getting up and away from a sedentary position can improve the quality and quantity of your life. One Australian study found that those who spend more than 10 hours a day in a sedentary state had a 46 per cent increased risk of premature death. It's a good idea to incorporate some yoga into your daily routine, to counteract the physical effects of remaining seated for so long. Poses such as Child Pose and Easy Seated Pose are good ways to stretch it out.

Learning to sit correctly and peacefully in the following postures is the first step in learning to calm your body and mind. While you're seated at your desk, you're exposed to constant visual stimulation. Remaining in a seated position in yoga, while remaining still, quiet and unstimulated, can be quite difficult for some. After practice it will become easier to assume this pose, and it will begin to act as a catalyst to switching off your mind.

Corpse Pose (Savasana)

This is the 'go to' pose when you're fatigued between postures, or during a relaxation phase. It's a wonderful recovery and calming position, which also helps to reduce stress levels and calm a busy mind.

1. **Lie flat** on your back, on the mat, with your arms and legs apart. Your legs should be around 60 centimetres apart, but do whatever is comfortable. Your toes should fall slightly outwards, so you'll feel a loosening in your lower back. You may need to shake your legs and shoulders a little to remove any stress or tension.

2. **Position your palms** facing upwards, fingers loosely curled.

3. **Gently roll** your head from side to side to release the neck area. Repeat this as many times as you need.

4. **Concentrate** on your breathing, using the deep breathing techniques mentioned on pages 222–28.

5. **If your neck feels** stiff, try relaxing your facial muscles. Soften the root of the tongue, and relax your gaze, so that you almost feel as though your eyes are sinking into your head. Try the facial relaxation exercise on page 207 (step 8).

6. **Hold** the Corpse Pose for at least five minutes to enter a state of complete relaxation.

Top Tip

If you're feeling tired, or have a headache or eyestrain, try staying in this pose for at least five minutes.

Child Pose (Balasana)

A wonderful stretch in its own right, Child Pose is a complete stretch for your spine, lower back and hips. Like its name, it's a warming and comforting pose, which helps to rejuvenate the nervous system.

1. **Kneel** on the floor and slowly lower yourself until your bottom is resting on your heels. Your big toes should be touching, but widen your knees to be hip-width apart.

2. **Breathe out** and lower your upper body towards your thighs. You should feel a strong stretch across your hips and lower back. Concentrate on this stretch, while lifting the base of your skull away from your neck.

1

Top Tip

Count to eight breaths before moving on to the next asana to ensure your body and mind are rested.

3. **If you can't quite stretch** all the way to the floor, rest your forehead onto folded arms.

4. **If you're comfortable** in this pose, place your arms alongside your upper body, palms up. You should feel a letting go of your shoulder blades. Relax into this.

5. **Hold** for up to three minutes. Use this pose to recover and rest whenever you need to.

Seated Staff Pose (Dandasana)

This deceptively easy-looking pose is the seated version of Mountain Pose. It looks simple, but can be difficult to hold for extended periods of time, especially if your core isn't particularly strong.

1. **Sit on your mat**, legs stretched out in front of you. Your upper body should be upright. Imagine a cord, which travels from the base of your spine through the top of your head. Whenever you feel yourself slouching, mentally tighten this cord. If you're having difficulty remaining in this pose, use a blanket or bolster to lift your pelvis off the floor, or sit against a wall to help your body find its natural alignment.

2. **Slightly adjust** your sitting position, so that you're perched mainly on the front of your sitting bones. Flex your feet towards you and harden your thighs. You should feel the backs of your knees press downwards onto the mat.

3. **Draw your thighs** towards your pelvis – do this with your thigh muscles, not your abdominals.

4. **Hold** this pose for up to one minute.

Top Tip

If your knees keep bending upwards, place a bolster or sandbag weights across your thighs to help keep them flat.

Easy Seated Pose (Sukhasana)

Sitting comfortably with your legs crossed tends to become more difficult as we get older, due to stiffness in our hips and loss of strength in our core. You'll need a blanket to help support your buttocks for this pose. This pose translates as 'happiness' – a good word to hold on to if you're finding it tough.

1. **Sit** on a folded blanket (it should be around 15 centimetres thick). Your sitting bones should be towards the edge of the blanket.

2. **Stretch your legs** out in front of you, following the same instructions for Seated Staff Pose (page 91).

3. **Cross your legs**, placing each foot comfortably under the opposite knee.

4. **Your legs should form a triangle**, its three sides formed by your two thighs and crossed shins.

5. **Check your posture**. If you're slumping forwards, or feel uncomfortable, readjust your sitting position. You may need to lift your bottom slightly off the blanket to do this.

6. **Place your hands** loosely in your lap, palms facing upwards, or you can choose to place your palms on your knees, gently cupping them.

7. **Hold** this position for as long as you can, then swap your legs over.

Lion Pose (Simhasana)

You may look (and feel) slightly ridiculous, but this is a perfect pose to relax facial muscles, reduce neck tension and relax your mind. It also opens up the area of communication (the throat).

1. **Kneel** on your mat, and cross your feet behind you. Start by crossing your right ankle over the back of your left one.

2. **Lower your bottom**, so that your perineum is on the top of your right heel. This should feel comfortable.

3. **Place your hands** firmly on your knees, or tops of your thighs. Splay your fingers (like a lion's claws).

4. **Inhale** through your nose. Then open your mouth as wide as you can, poke your tongue out, down towards your chin, and widen the splay of your fingers. Don't slouch over to do this.

5. **Open your eyes wide** and exhale, making a 'ha' sound from the back of your throat. Focus on your nose or the space between your eyebrows, whichever feels more comfortable.

6. **Repeat** the roar two or three times. If you feel embarrassed, just keep roaring until you feel loosened and relaxed.

7. **Reverse** your legs and repeat.

4

Head-To-Knee Pose (Janu Sirsasana)

This pose is a good way to help relieve anxieties and fears, and reduce stress. Remember to breathe deeply and evenly – this will help calm you.

1. **Sit down** on your mat, with your legs stretched out in front of you. Sit on the edge of a folded blanket if you need to.

2. **Inhale** and bring your right foot back towards your perineum, bending your knee. Your right foot should be next to your inner left thigh.

3. **Place the sole of your right foot** against your inner left thigh by allowing your right knee to drop to the floor. Your right shin should be at a right angle to your left leg. If your right knee doesn't reach the floor, place a blanket or bolster under your knee to support it.

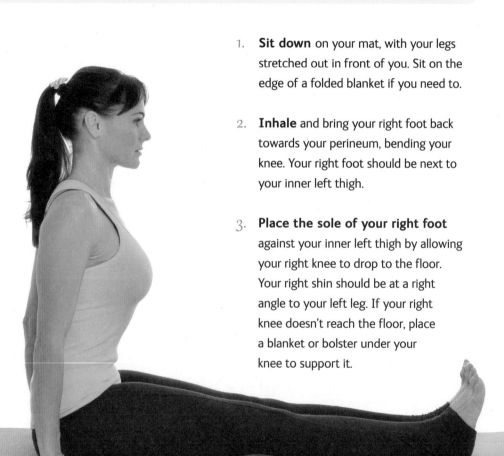

4. **Place your palms on the floor** either side of your left leg.

5. **Exhale** and lift your upper body slightly upwards as you bend forwards, turning your torso to the left as you do so. Your belly button should line up with the centre of your left thigh and kneecap. If you don't feel comfortable, or would like to increase this stretch, place a strap around your left foot. Make sure that you're leaning forwards from your hips, not your shoulders when you hold the strap.

6. **If you can, slowly grab** hold of your left foot with your right hand. Your thumb should be on the sole of your foot, your fingers placed near your toes.

7. **Inhale** and lift your torso, strengthening the left thigh by pressing it into the floor and extending through your left heel. If you need to increase the twist, place your left hand beside your left hip.

4

8. **When you've twisted your torso** as far as you can, grab the outside of your left foot with your left hand. Your arms should be fully extended, both firmly grasping your left foot.

9. **Exhale** and extend your torso forwards, making sure that the stretch comes from your groin, not your hips or shoulders. Your elbows will naturally lift out to the sides. Increase your stretch as much as you comfortably can, until your belly is touching your thighs and your head is as close to your shin as possible.

10. **Hold** this pose for up to one minute. As you practise, and become more flexible, build your stretch up to three minutes.

11. **Slowly roll back** to upright position. Swap sides and repeat.

Seated Forward Bend (Paschimottanasana)

Also known as Double-Leg Forward Stretch, this is an emotional as well as physical pose, which allows you to let go of deep-seated stress, emotions, frustrations and resentment. It can also help to reduce body fat, as it stimulates your abdominals.

1. **Sit down** on your mat, with your legs stretched out in front of you. Sit on the edge of a folded blanket if you need to.

2. **Press firmly down** through your heels and rock gently side to side. This allows you to adjust the sitting bones correctly on the mat.

3. **Use your hands** if necessary to turn the tops of your thighs towards the floor, pressing your thighs downwards as you do so.

4. **Place your hands** or fingertips on either side of your hips. As you press firmly downwards through your hands, lift the top of your sternum towards the ceiling.

5. **Imagine** your groin pulling backwards into your pelvis.

6. **Inhale**, and lean forwards, making sure to stretch your torso from your hips, not your waist. Avoid bending at the waist, by lifting your upper torso upwards before bending forwards.

7. **If you can, hold** the sides of your feet with your hands, thumbs on the soles of your feet, elbows fully extended outwards. (If you can't reach this far, use a strap to pull your torso forwards, but keep your elbows bent.)

8. **To increase the stretch**, lift your torso slightly and stretch forwards, through your upper body. Don't use the strap or your hands for this. Your lower body should be just touching your upper thighs. As you increase the stretch with each exhalation, your diaphragm, chest and head should then rest on your legs. The goal is to stretch your arms beyond your feet, but don't worry if this seems impossible for now!

9. **Hold** this pose for at least one minute. As you practise, slowly increase this time to three minutes.

10. **To return to the starting position**, slowly peel your head, chest, and belly up from your thighs. Straighten your elbows, then inhale and return to neutral by pulling your tailbone downwards into your pelvis, as though you're tucking your bottom under.

7

Hero Pose (Virasana)

One of the basic seated poses, this is a good opener for your hips and lower back. If you experience back pain at the end of the day, or during menstruation, try this pose for some relief. It's also a counter pose to the Lotus Posture (page 119).

1. **Kneel** on your mat, with your knees slightly touching. Slide your feet outwards, until they're a little further than hip-width apart. Press the tops of your feet firmly downwards, and angle your big toes towards each other.

2. **Exhale** and move your body down and back until you're sitting between your feet. If this is uncomfortable, and it probably will be for beginners, place a blanket under your knees, shins and feet. Rest your hands on top of your thighs and lean your upper torso slightly forward.

3. **If you can't sit** easily on the floor, place a block between your feet. Sit straight, with your sitting bones resting evenly on the floor or block. Your chest and upper body should be strong, slightly towards the ceiling. You should feel an opening across your chest.

4. **Check** your shoulder blades. They should be away from your ears, opened across and down your back.

5. **Hold** this pose for 30 seconds, slowly building up to one minute. As you practise, work up to holding this pose for five minutes. You probably won't need the props as you become stronger.

6. **To return to the starting position**, press your hands on the floor in front of you, and slightly lift your bottom away from your heels. Cross your ankles, sit onto the floor behind your feet, bringing your legs in front of you.

Top Tip

When you've returned to neutral, bounce your legs up and down a few times to release any muscle strain.

Heron Pose (Krounchasana)

If you suffer from stiff hamstrings, or have noticed that they're sore and stiff after exercise, take the time to practise this pose. You may not be able to completely raise your leg on your first attempts, so use a strap or belt around the sole of your foot to help you.

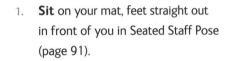

1. **Sit** on your mat, feet straight out in front of you in Seated Staff Pose (page 91).

2. **Bring your left leg back** so that it's tucked in next to your body (as if going into Hero Pose). The top of your left foot and shin should rest on the floor; toes should be pointing straight back.

3. **Bend your right knee** and bring the right foot down on the floor in front of your right buttock.

4. **Lift the right foot**, holding on to it with both hands. Lean back slightly, but keep your chest lifted, and pull your shoulder blades down and across your back.

5. **Inhale** and raise your leg until it's at a 45-degree angle with the floor. Your foot should be slightly higher than your head.

6. **Check your posture** and make sure that you're not slumping over to achieve this stretch. If you are, breathe out and, on your inhalation, try to elongate your torso.

7. **Hold** for up to 30 seconds, slowly working your way up to one minute.

8. **To return to the starting point**, keep hold of your right foot and exhale, returning it flat to the floor. Straighten both legs and repeat the steps on the other side.

Gate Pose (Parighasana)

This is a great pose to stretch your side muscles and improve your respiratory function. If this pose hurts your knees, or is painful, use another mat or a blanket to support your bottom and hips.

1. **Kneel** on your mat.

2. **Stretch your right leg** directly out to the right, keeping your foot firmly pressed into the floor.

3. **Check your posture**. Your left hip should be directly above your left knee; make sure you haven't shifted your posture.

4. **Concentrate** on your pelvic area. Turn it slightly to the right – your left hip should shift towards the right a little. Your upper body should still be facing forwards.

5

5. **Turn your right kneecap** towards the ceiling, so that your leg turns outwards. Your foot should be flat on the floor, pointing outwards.

6. **Inhale**, and allow your arms to hang softly at your sides, palms facing downwards. Bend to the right over your right leg, stretching your right hand down your leg as you do so. You can rest your hand on the floor if you need to.

7. **Feel the stretch** along your left side. In a circular movement, reach upwards with your left arm, until your arm is behind your left ear. This will automatically propel your torso forwards, so use your left hip to maintain your position.

8. **Hold** this stretch for 30 seconds, slowly working your way up to one minute.

9. **Inhale** and return to the starting position, using your left arm to propel the movement. Bring your knees together and repeat on the opposite side.

Top Tip

If you have knee injuries or problems, perform this pose seated on a chair.

Seated-Angle Pose (Upavista Konasana)

Also known as Open-Angle Pose, this posture opens the entire groin and hip area, which releases tension in the lower back, making it a good therapeutic pose for those with sciatica.

1. **Begin in Seated Staff Pose** (page 91), seated upright. If you find this difficult, sit on a folded blanket to lift your pelvis and hips.

2. **Place your hands** behind you and lean backwards on them (very slightly). Open your legs as wide as you can, to around 90 degrees. With your hands still behind you, shift your buttocks forwards. This will help you stretch your legs further.

3. **Press your outer thighs** down firmly, which will turn your thighs slightly inwards. Your kneecaps should be facing the ceiling, legs stretched through your heels. Concentrate on stretching through your heels, as this will keep your knees steady.

Top Tip

Having trouble bending forwards? Bend your knees slightly, keeping your kneecaps facing the ceiling.

4. **Keep your thighs** pressed firmly downwards, and slowly lean forwards, walking your hands between your legs towards your feet. Check your posture and make sure you're bending forwards from your hips, not your waist.

5. **With each exhalation**, stretch a little further.

6. **Hold** this pose for at least one minute. As you return to upright position, ensure that your torso is long and lean.

Seated Side Stretch
(Parsva Upavista Konasana)

Open your hip area and release tension in the backs of your thighs with a side stretch. If it's difficult, place a rolled-up blanket on your thighs to aid your pose. It is easier to perform the move with legs crossed, as here. This will help you maintain the pose so that you can receive the full benefits.

1. **Begin in Seated Staff Pose** (page 91).

2. **Bring your legs** up so that your legs are crossed.

Top Tip

Avoid this pose if you have or experience pain in the lower back, legs or hips.

3. **Place your left palm** on the floor, as close as possible to your left buttock and hip. Your fingers should be pointed outwards.

4. **Inhale and lift** your right arm above your head, palm facing inwards.

5. **Exhale and stretch** towards the left side of the mat – your left hand will slide slightly outwards.

6. **Make sure** that your bottom is evenly and firmly sitting on the floor. Keep your back straight – imagine that there is a string connecting your head to the ceiling.

7. **If you can**, turn your head to look past your right elbow.

8. **Stay here** for as long as you can – ideally up to one minute.

9. **Repeat** steps 2 to 8 for the left arm.

Cobbler's Pose (Baddha Konasana)

The benefits of this pose are many. It's ideal for those suffering from PMT, or going through the menopause; it relieves back pain; lowers blood pressure; reduces anxiety, depression and fatigue; and is recommended for pregnant women to help relieve childbirth pain.

1. **Sit** comfortably with your legs straight out in front of you. If your hips and groin are tight, sit on a folded blanket to relieve pain and pressure.

2. **Exhale and bend** your knees, pulling your feet towards your pelvis. Place the soles of your feet together, and drop your knees out to the sides.

3. **Take hold** of your big toes with your thumb and first and second fingers,

Top Tip

If this pose hurts your sacral area, then adjust your blanket so that you're sitting higher off the ground.

open the toes and spread your soles wide, then hold the feet with both hands interlaced around them. If you can't reach that far, hold your ankle or shin. Your pelvis should be neutral, so that your perineum is fixed to the floor.

4. **Hold your upper body** upright and strong. You should feel your chest area lift, and your shoulder blades slide slightly down your back.

5. **Hold** this pose for one minute, slowly building up to five minutes.

6. **Inhale**, raising your knees up to meet, and stretch your legs out in front of you.

3

Reclining Bound-Angle Pose (Supta Baddha Konasana)

This is a natural progression from Cobbler's Pose, further opening the hip and groin area. You may need to experiment with bolsters and padding to ensure your comfort, but once you're in it's a wonderful position for relaxation.

1. **Repeat** the steps for Cobbler's Pose (page 109).

2. **Exhale** and lower your upper body backwards towards the floor. Use your hands to support this move.

3. **Lean** on your hands, then lower yourself onto your forearms. As you do so, place your hands onto your lower back and bottom, simultaneously resting on your forearms and hands. Firmly but gently, use your hands to spread and release this area.

⑦

4. **Lower your torso**
    to the floor. If this is
    painful or places too much strain
    on your lower back or hips, rest on
    a rolled-up blanket or bolster.

5. **Allow your legs to fall open.** Gently
    rotate your inner thighs outwards with
    your hands. Gently press your thighs to
    increase the width of the stretch.

6. **Place your hands** onto your hip bones
    (the point that you can feel through
    your skin). Gently push these towards
    each other. This helps to widen the
    pelvis across the back.

7. **Relax your arms**, keeping them
    around 45 degrees at either side of
    your body. Remain here for up to one
    minute. As you become used to the
    stretch and more confident and
    comfortable, you may be able to
    maintain this pose for up to 10 minutes.

Top Tip

**Don't press down onto your knees
to create a bigger stretch in your
thighs and groin. Your knees should
remain soft and the stretch should
come from your pelvis.**

Garland Pose (Malasana)

While this pose focuses on stretching and opening the thigh area, it will also tone your belly and strengthen your stomach muscles. If you find it difficult, sit on the edge of a chair and follow the steps.

1. **Stand** on your mat, and lower your body into a squat. Your feet should be close together, heels raised off the floor.

Top Tip

Want to increase your stretch? From step 5, continue to press your inner thighs against your upper body. Reach either side of your feet, so that your armpits are resting on your shins. Grasp the outside of your ankles until you can grab hold of the back of your heels, or press your fingertips onto the floor.

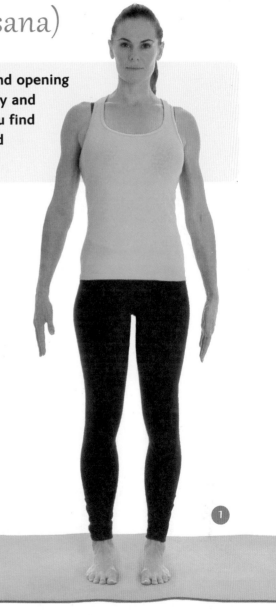

1

2. **Widen your thighs**, so that your kneecaps are wider than your waist.

3. **Exhale** and lean forward, so that your torso is positioned between your thighs. Lower the heels flat to the floor.

4. **Press your elbows** against either knee, fitting your elbow into the soft area inside your knee.

5. **Bring your palms together** in Anjali Mudra (Salutation Seal). Your knees should be resisting against your elbows. Feel your torso strengthen and lengthen.

6. **Hold** the position for 30 seconds to a minute.

7. **Inhale**, straighten your knees, raise your torso and return to a standing position.

Cow-Face Pose (Gomukhasana)

An amusing name for a relatively difficult posture. Cow-Face Pose has nothing to do with your facial expression, but everything to do with stretching and opening your chest area. Ideal for those with respiratory issues.

1. **Begin in Seated Staff Pose** (page 91). Bend your knees upwards, so that your feet are firmly placed on the floor.

2. **Slowly slide your left foot** under your right knee, so that your left heel is close to the right hip.

3. **Cross your right leg** over the left. Your right knee should 'hug' your left knee. You can use your hands to bring your left heel closer to your right hip. Your heels should be parallel to each other.

4. **Check your posture**. You should be sitting evenly on your sitting bones.

5. **Inhale** and stretch your left arm to the left, in line with your shoulder.

6. **Rotate your palm** so that your thumb leads the movement. Continue to turn until your palm is facing the ceiling and your hand is pointing behind you.

7. **Exhale** and continue the movement, until your arm is behind your waist, resting on, or parallel to it. Your left elbow should be against your left side.

8. **Slide your forearm** up your spine, so that your fingertips are facing the base of your neck. Your left elbow should still be against the left side of your torso.

9. **Inhale** and reach with your right arm until it's pointing forwards, palm facing downwards. Turn your palm over, and stretch towards the ceiling, turning your palm to face behind you.

10. **Exhale** and bend at your elbow to meet your left hand. If you can, clasp your fingers or hook them together.

11. **Increase the stretch** by continuing to point and raise your right elbow towards the ceiling, while directing your left elbow downwards to the floor. Make sure your right arm is pressed against the right side of your head.

12. **Hold** this pose for about one minute. Release your arms and legs, and repeat on the other side.

Sage Pose (Marichyasana)

This posture means 'ray of light'. You may have difficulty achieving the full reach for this pose, but don't be discouraged and continue to embrace the stretch. Every time you practise this pose, you'll find that you stretch a little further.

1. **Begin in Seated Staff Pose** (page 91). Bring your right knee towards your torso by placing your right foot on the floor, close to your bottom.

2. **Make your left leg strong** by pressing the left heel into the floor. Rotate your upper thigh inwards.

3. **Breathe out** and turn your upper body to the right. Place your left arm on the outside of the right thigh and place your right palm on the floor behind your back.

4. **Check your posture**: make sure that your left leg is strong and straight and your right foot is firmly pressed into the ground.

5. **Continue stretching** your spine a little more with each inhalation, and twisting with each exhalation.

6. **Gently turn your head** to the right and try to look back, to complete the twist in your cervical spine.

7. **Hold** this pose for 30 seconds to one minute. Exhale and return your torso to the centre. Swap legs and twist to the left.

Top Tip

If you find that your back hunches, or you can't stay upright when you twist your torso, sit on a blanket to help keep your pelvis in a neutral position.

6

Lotus Pose (Padmasana)

This pose is the one most associated with yoga – it represents calm and clarity, just like the lotus flower the position is meant to represent. It opens up the hip area as well as creating flexibility in the knees and ankles. It can take some time until you achieve the full stretch, so keep persevering.

1. **Sit on the floor** with your legs stretched straight out in front of you.

2. **Bend your right knee** and draw the heel of the right foot into the inner thigh of the left leg.

3. **Maintaining** this angle, lift your ankle and knee with both hands. Place the instep of your right foot onto the left hip crease.

4. **Bend the left knee** until the left foot is under the right shin. Then bring the left knee slightly out to the side while keeping the leg bent.

5. **Gently lift the left foot towards** the right hip crease. Keep your knees soft and do not squeeze your legs.

6. **Open your hips** as fully as you can.

7. **Hold** this position for at least one minute, maintaining it for as long as you can. As you become more experienced, this is the ideal pose for meditation.

⑤

Top Tip

Each time you practise this pose, change the leg you place first. This will help you become more balanced in the posture.

Downward-Facing Dog Pose (Adho Mukha Svanasana)

Possibly one of the best-known and popular poses, Downward-Facing Dog Pose forms part of the Sun Salutation sequence (page 196). On its own, it's a great upper body stretch – lenthening and stretching the back, shoulders and upper body – so perfect after a long day sitting at your desk.

1. **Rest on your hands and knees** on your mat. Your knees should be directly below your hips, and your hands slightly forwards from your shoulders.

Top Tip

If you can't reach this stretch, try lightening the pose by bending your knees in towards your chest.

6

2. **Spread your palms**, and turn your toes under.

3. **Exhale** and lift your bottom upwards, so that your knees come away from the floor. Keep your knees slightly bent.

4. **Lift and lengthen your tailbone** away from your pelvis, while simultaneously lifting your sitting bones upwards.

5. **Strengthen** the inside of your thighs and calves, concentrating on drawing them all the way up to your groin.

6. **Exhale** and push the top of your thighs backwards. Lower your heels, straightening the legs and keeping the high upward rotation of the sitting bones.

7. **Hold** the pose for five breaths.

8. **Return to Child Pose** (page 89) and rest for eight breaths. Repeat five times.

Top Tip

It's very easy to overextend or sway your back with this pose, which can lead to lower back problems. Your stretch should be through your arms and shoulders, not your back.

Plank Pose (Kumbhakasana)

Part of the Sun Salutation sequence (page 196), this posture focuses on building a strong core, which is imperative to good physical health. It will tone your abdominal muscles and also your wrists as they hold the weight of your body. It is nicely countered by the East Stretch Pose (page 158).

1. **Begin in Downward-Facing Dog Pose** (page 120).

Top Tip

To advance this pose, try lifting one leg at a time. Keep the rest of your body as still as possible, and don't swing your hips.

1

2. **Inhale** and pull your torso forwards until your arms are perpendicular to the floor and the shoulders are positioned directly over the wrists, and your torso is parallel to the floor.

3. **Press the forearms and hands** firmly into the floor. Check your posture, and do not let your chest sink towards the floor. Strengthen your lower back and legs by pressing firmly down through the heels.

4. **Your neck and spine should be straight**, eyes directed to your mat, your thighs pulled upwards.

Make sure your neck isn't tense. Take some deep breaths if you're feeling any tension around your throat and shoulders.

5. **Hold** this position for up to one minute.

Top Tip

It's important to keep your back flat, so ask a friend or the instructor to check for you.

Four-Limbed Staff Pose (Chaturanga Dandasana)

Another part of the Sun Salutation sequence (page 196), this pose requires strength to maintain a strong body while you lower it to the floor. It's also a good toner for your upper arm muscles.

1. **Perform a Downward-Facing Dog Pose** (page 120), followed by a Plank Pose (page 122).

Top Tip

While this pose is part of the Sun Salutation sequence, you can try doing this pose on its own, holding it for at least 30 seconds.

2. **In Plank Pose**, slowly lower your body on an exhalation. Make sure that your body is even, your chest hasn't lowered and your bottom hasn't risen towards the ceiling. Focus on your belly button and draw it back through to your spine.

3. **With your elbows tucked in** neatly at the side, press firmly through your hands. Raise your head slightly, fixing your gaze in front of you.

4. **Either lower your body** to the mat to rest, or return to Downward-Facing Dog and repeat the two steps.

Twists and Abdominal Toners

When you think of rock-hard defined abs, you might imagine hours of sit-ups, weights and dieting. Strong stomach muscles are entirely achievable through yoga. These postures tone us internally too. In twists, the organs are compressed, pushing out blood containing metabolic by-products and toxins. When we release the twist, fresh blood flows in, carrying oxygen and nutrients for tissue healing.

Making The Reach

Full range of motion in spinal rotation is essential to many yoga poses. Unfortunately, many people lose full spinal rotation in the course of living a sedentary lifestyle. If you do not lengthen the muscles, tendons, ligaments and fascia (connective tissue) to their full length at least a few times a week, they will gradually shorten and limit the nearby joints' mobility.

The Value Of Twists

From a physiological standpoint, twists stimulate circulation and have a cleansing and refreshing effect on the organs and associated glands. They improve the suppleness of the diaphragm, and relieve spinal, hip and groin disorders. The spine also becomes more supple, and this improves the flow of blood to the spinal nerves and increases energy levels.

Strengthening Your Core

Another reason to concentrate on strengthening your stomach muscles is to create a stable core for your body. Your core is made up of the muscles around your spine and pelvis – transversus abdominis, internal and external obliques, erector spinae, etc. With a weakened core, you're more likely to suffer from lower back pain, sciatica, hip pain and reduced movement. Yoga is designed to strengthen your stomach muscles, which in turn means you'll have a better stability of the skeletal system and reduced back pain.

Targeting The Tummy

We've already shown many of the ways that yoga can reduce stress. But what's stress got to do with your belly? Almost everything. When we're stressed, our bodies tend to store fat around our middle – particularly in women. It then becomes a Catch-22 – the more stressed we get, the bigger our bellies become. The bigger our bellies become, the more we stress about getting rid of our tummy fat.

Double Leg Raises (Urdhva Prasarita Padasana)

This posture strengthens a muscle that passes through the very core of your body, which aids your posture, your movement and even (because this muscle is in close proximity to the back of the diaphragm) the way you breathe. This pose is wonderful for reducing fat round the abdomen, strengthening the lumbar region of the back, and toning the abdominal organs.

1. **Lie** on your mat with your legs slightly apart, palms facing up.

2. **Take some deep breaths** in and out. On an in breath, contract your pelvic floor muscle, draw your belly button towards your spine and raise both your legs up together, with your kneecaps drawn up, keeping your legs straight. Keep your lower back on the floor with your tailbone down, trying not to bend your knees or lift your bottom off the mat.

3. **Momentarily hold** at your highest possible point before slowly lowering your legs to the mat, keeping them level.

2

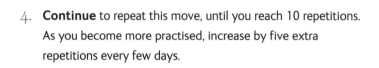

4. **Continue** to repeat this move, until you reach 10 repetitions. As you become more practised, increase by five extra repetitions every few days.

5. **ADVANCED MOVE**: When you lower your legs, don't take them all the way down but keep them a few centimetres above the mat, before lifting again. Repeat.

②

Benefits Recap

 **Strengthens lower back and psoas muscles**

✅ **Tones abdominal muscles**

✅ **Improves posture**

Top Tip

If you suffer from back pain, sciatica, knee pain or back problems, do not attempt this move.

③

Boat Pose (Navasana)

Despite the effort and many actions involved, finding stability in this posture can help calm and align your body, mind and emotions. This asana helps strengthen the abdomen, the hip flexors and the spine and back muscles. This also brings about the stimulation of kidney, thyroid, prostate and the intestines.

1. **Sit** on your mat with your legs straight in front of you. Ensure that you're perched on your sitting bones.

2. **Place your hands** either side of you, beside your hips, fingers towards your feet. Your arms should be strong and straight.

3. **Breathe out** and bend your knees, lifting your feet from the mat so that your thighs are at a 45-degree angle to the mat. Focus on your pubic bone, and lift it slightly towards your belly button.

4. **Raise your arms** so that they are parallel to each other and to the floor. If

you're having problems doing this, keep your fingers splayed either side of your hips.

5. **Breathe in**, then exhale and lift your lower legs, so that your toes are level with your gaze. If this is too difficult, keep your legs bent.

6. **If your arms are raised**, make sure that your shoulder blades are down and open across your back.

7. **Reach forwards**, keeping your torso long and strong.

8. **Check** your stomach muscles – make sure that they haven't tensed. Breathe, and draw your belly button back towards your spine, while lifting your chest towards the ceiling. Don't raise your gaze any further than your toes to avoid too much stress on your neck and shoulders.

9. **Try to hold** for at least 10 seconds, gradually building – in 10-second increments – to one minute. Relax with each exhalation and draw your upper body upwards with each inhalation.

Revolved Easy Pose (Parivrtta Sukhasana)

This pose will improve your digestion and detox your system by stimulating the agni (digestive fire) in the belly and boosting the performance of the liver and kidneys. It also energizes the spine, relieves fatique, sciatica and backache, helps with anxiety, stress and tension, as well as stretching the shoulders, hips and neck.

1. **Sit** with your bottom on the edge of a folded blanket. If you find this difficult, sit on a yoga bolster or block.

2. **Cross your legs** into Easy Seated Pose (page 92). Ensure that your weight is distributed evenly across your sitting bones. Keep the sitting bones firmly anchored and the pelvis still. Check that your head, neck and spine are in a straight line. Extend your spine upwards without tensing your neck.

2

3. **Place your left hand** around 30 centimetres behind your left hip. Then, bring your right hand onto the outside of your left knee, resting it, not pulling the knee forwards.

4. **Gently turn** your body towards the left with some rotation in the pelvis allowing for movement in the twist. Keep your gaze over your left shoulder and hand.

5. **When you are firmly anchored**, you need to achieve even more lift through the pelvic floor to avoid stressing the lumbar spine and creating problems in the sacrum. Ensure that your pelvic muscles are engaged and your belly button is pulled towards your spine.

6. **Check your posture.** Make sure you're not slouching by keeping the sternum lifted and your collarbones spread. Relax your shoulders down.

7. **Hold** this pose for 10 breaths.

8. **Breathe out**, then return to the centre. Change your legs, and repeat the twist on the other side.

4

Half Spinal Twist (Ardha Matsyendrasana)

Also known as 'Lord of the Fish Pose' – in Sanskrit *ardha* means 'half', *matsya* means 'fish' and *endra* means 'lord'. This position tones the spinal nerves and ligaments, and improves digestion and the reproductive systems by massaging internal organs, particularly the liver and spleen.

1. **Begin** in Seated Staff Pose (page 91).

2. **Bend your right knee**, keeping your right foot flat on the floor outside your left thigh.

3. **Bend your left leg** under your right leg to bring your left heel to the outside of your right buttock and let the left leg sit on the floor to the right of your right foot.

4. **Check your posture**. Make sure both sitting bones are planted firmly on the mat and your upper body is upright. You can sit on a folded blanket to ensure you get the lift from the bottom of the spine.

5. **Place your right arm** directly behind you, fingers facing outwards.

6. **Place your left arm** around your right knee, gently pulling your thigh towards the centreline of the body.

7. **Take a deep breath**. On the out breath, slowly and gently twist your upper body to the right, sitting upright, by pressing down into the sitting bones, and keeping the abdomen soft. Lift and lengthen the spine.

Top Tip

This posture is ideal for stretching and increasing the flexibility of the spine. Try performing it first thing in the morning and again before bed.

6

8. **Bring the left arm up** and rest the upper arm on the outside of your right knee, with your hand in the air.

9. **When you've twisted** as far as you comfortably can, turn your head to look over your right shoulder. (If you suffer from neck or shoulder pain, or experience any pain during this, keep your focus straight ahead and don't twist your head.)

10. **Focus** on the lift of the spine and the twist all the way from the base of the spine to the very top of the cranium.

11. **Hold** this pose for around 30 seconds, over time building up to a minute.

12. **Repeat** on the other side.

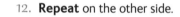

Caution

Avoid this pose during your period or if you are pregnant. If you have neck issues, do not turn the neck. Be careful if you have a back or spinal injury. Finally, if you have sore knees, keep the bottom leg straight.

Revolved Abdomen Pose (Jathara Parivartanasana)

Pep up your mind and body after a day's work with this pose. Performing this posture after a long day can help you get rid of emotional fatigue and bring balance to your mind and body.

1. **Lie** on your mat, with knees bent and feet flat on the ground. Your knees should be around 45 degrees to the floor.

2. **If your neck feels tense** or painful, place a pillow under your head.

3. **Exhale**, and bring your knees to your chest. Grab your knees in a hugging motion, pulling them towards you.

4. **Release your knees**, place your arms out to either side onto the floor, palms facing down.

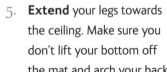

5. **Extend** your legs towards the ceiling. Make sure you don't lift your bottom off the mat and arch your back.

6

6. **On an out breath**, bring both legs towards the right, down towards the floor. Your left hip will lift slightly off the mat. Perform this move slowly, so that your legs fall slowly and smoothly towards the ground, until your legs and upper body are at a 90-degree angle, keeping both shoulders flat to the floor. Try to keep your spine straight from the pelvic floor pubis area all the way up to the crown of your head.

7. **Keep your shoulders** relaxed and away from your ears. Sometimes the shoulder on one side of the body gets lifted during the twist. Relax the shoulder back and make sure both are grounded equally.

Top Tip

Had a big meal? Try doing this pose around 30 minutes after eating to help improve digestion.

6

8. **Reach your right foot**, if you can, and grab hold of your toes with your right hand to increase the stretch. Use a yoga strap if you can't reach your toes.

9. **Slowly turn your head** to your left hand and allow your gaze to rest on your fingertips.

10. **Hold** this position for 10 seconds, over time building up to 25 seconds.

11. **Inhale**, and return your feet to the centre, so that your feet are facing the ceiling again.

12. **Bend your knees** and hug them to your chest.

13. **Exhale**, and stretch your feet towards the ceiling again. Repeat the above steps on the other side.

Pendant Pose (Lolasana)

This pose strengthens wrists, tones upper arms, develops your abdominal muscles and works your back muscles. You will also feel an exhilaration and sense of accomplishment if you actually manage to defy gravity and take flight. Be careful if you have any wrist, shoulder or neck problems, and avoid this pose if you have pain in the finger joints.

1. **Kneel** on the mat, sitting on your heels with legs together, and your hands flat on the floor by your side. Use blocks to reach the floor if you have short arms.

Top Tip

This is an easy way to firm up those 'bingo' wings. You'll also strengthen your wrists and abdominal muscles. Blocks give extra height to make the lift a little easier.

2. **Slide forwards** to kneel on your mat on all fours, with your palms still flat against the floor or blocks. Your knees should be directly below your hips, your stomach muscles relaxed but strong. Your hands should be slightly in front of your shoulders.

3. **Exhale**, and tip your tailbone towards the floor and slightly forwards. Your back should be arched towards the ceiling, and your chin tucked in towards your chest. Feel the stretch from your head to your tailbone.

4. **Spread** your shoulder blades. Keep your arms firm and cross your ankles. Press your hands into the floor/blocks.

5. **Tuck your torso** in and lift your knees up, bending your legs (keeping ankles crossed) into a tight ball, then raise the ball by pulling the navel towards your spine and closing the space between your pubis and sternum.

6. **Keep your upper back rounded** by stretching your shoulder blades as far away from your spine as you can. Stretch for 10 to 15 seconds.

7. **Exhale**, and return to neutral position and cross your legs the other way.

Top Tip

If you can't lift your whole weight at first, just practise lifting your knees up as high as you can without taking your ankles off the floor.

Back-Bending Postures

Around 85 per cent of the world's population is affected by back pain. According to the World Health Organization (WHO), more people are disabled by musculoskeletal disorders (MSDs) – especially back pain – than any other group of diseases. Yet back pain, which incidentally costs individuals and businesses billions of dollars each year due to sickness and consultations, could easily be reduced through exercise, proper stretching and, of course, yoga.

How Yoga Benefits Your Back

Yoga works to correct your posture. Misaligned posture can cause issues with your upper and lower back, as well as other skeletal problems. Aligning your posture involves improving the balance between muscle length and muscle strength.

Yoga does this perfectly, because, when you hold an asana and then practise its opposite or counter pose, the major muscles on both the front and back of the body are both stretched and strengthened.

It's not just our muscles we need to attend to, but also the connective tissue (fasciae) between them. Yoga is of great benefit to the fasciae that are crucial to movement but require care. While muscles are relatively robust and can withstand stretching or pressure applied during exercise or lifting objects, fasciae need gentler treatment.

Why We Have Back Pain

Constant misuse of muscles and fasciae, through poor posture, carrying objects incorrectly, wearing the wrong footwear, or even performing stretches incorrectly, hardens the fasciae and holds your muscles in a potentially pain-inducing position.

The following poses are all designed to help you correct your posture and create skeletal strength. When dealing with your back, take it slowly and do not try to push through the pain. Remember, yoga is not a race.

Locust Pose (Salabhasana)

A preparation pose which readies the back for the back stretching and backbends you're about to do.

1. **Lie face down**, with your arms at your sides. If you need to, place a folded blanket under your pelvis, hips and ribs.

2. **Your palms** should be facing upwards, your forehead on the floor.

3. **Turn your big toes** towards each other. You should feel your thighs rotate inwards and your bottom muscles should be tense. Your pelvis will feel the pressure from your coccyx; adjust your blanket if needed.

4. **Exhale**, and lift your head, upper torso, arms and legs away from the floor. Stretch your lower body so that you feel the strength of your stretch right through to your toes.

Top Tip

This is great for strengthening the back. Perform Locust Pose if your posture needs improving, or you've spent the day at a desk.

1

5. **Raise your arms** upwards towards the ceiling, palms facing downwards. Continue to lift upwards.

6. **Check** the posture of your head. You should be looking straight ahead, so that your neck is long.

7. **Hold** this position for 30 seconds to one minute, and release on an out breath. Repeat a few more times.

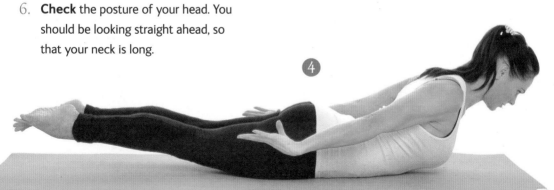

Cobra Pose (Bhujangasana)

Increase your energy levels (sexual and emotional) with this upper body stretch. Take your time with this pose – it's an exhilarating and awakening feeling.

1. **Lie on your front** on your mat, with your arms by your sides, feet stretched outwards so that the tops of your feet are flat to the floor.

2. **Place your hands** on the floor, just under your shoulders, so that your elbows are facing just behind you.

3. **Press your feet**, thighs and pubic bone into the floor.

4. **Breathe out**, and push yourself upwards, so that your upper body is off the mat, hips still connecting with the floor. Your tailbone should be pressing the pubic area downwards and towards your belly button. Don't tense your thighs or bottom.

5. **Lift your chest** and sternum forwards and upwards. Check that you haven't tensed your lower back.

6. **Hold** for 15 to 30 seconds, breathing slowly and steadily.

7. **Return** to the starting position, and repeat several times.

4

Upward-Facing Dog Pose (Urdhva Mukha Svanasana)

This pose will probably feel familiar to many, as it's part of the Sun Salutation (page 196) series of movements. You can practise it on its own to strengthen your upper body, especially the lower back.

1. **Lie on your front** on your mat. Stretch your legs, reaching backwards, and point your toes, resting the tops of your feet on the mat.

2. **Place your arms** on either side of your waist, so that your elbows are bent, facing towards the ceiling, and your palms are flat on the floor.

3. **Slow your breathing** and, on the in breath, push downwards through your hands. You should feel as though you're about to pull your body forwards.

Top Tip

This is a good move to do before starting work on a Monday, as it helps to relieve low-lying depression.

4. **Inhale**, then straighten your arms, while lifting your upper body off the floor. The tops of your thighs should also be about five centimetres off the floor.

5. **Check** your arms and legs (or ask somebody to). Your thighs should be slightly turned inwards – turn your big toes towards each other to help achieve this. Your arms should be turning inwards, so that the insides of your elbows are pointing towards the top of your mat.

6. **Push** your lower body towards your belly button. While your bottom muscles shouldn't be tensed, your hips should remain narrow.

7. **Lift** your sternum slightly, making sure that your shoulder blades are low and open across your back.

8. **Fix your gaze** to a point at eye level in front of you. Don't look up towards the ceiling, as this can compress your neck muscles.

9. **Hold** for 15 to 30 seconds before returning to the floor.

10. **After a few repetitions**, move into Downward-Facing Dog Pose (page 120) on an out breath.

Crocodile Pose (Makrasana)

This is a difficult pose, but one that will become easier with time. It's worth persevering, as it helps to stretch and strengthen your torso.

1. **Lie** on your front with your arms by your sides.

2. **Exhale**, and lift your head and upper torso upwards using your core muscles to lift. If you don't have lower back problems, move your legs slightly away from each other. Many people find it easier to keep their legs together to reduce lower-back strain.

3. **Your stomach muscles** should be firm and strong. If you experience any lower-back pain, stop immediately and return to the starting position. Your lower ribs, abdomen and pelvis should be anchored to the mat. If this feels painful, try placing another mat under your body.

4. **Bring the arms forwards** and fold
them. Then place the forehead on the
folded elbows and relax the neck.

5. **Remain here** for up to 30 seconds.
As you become more practised and
your strength improves, extend this
to one minute.

6. **Return** to the starting position
and repeat a few times.

Top Tip

If you have neck problems
or injuries, place a blanket
under your forehead and keep
your forehead resting on it
throughout the move.

Crescent-Moon Pose (Anjaneyasana)

Also known as Salutation Pose, this energizing posture helps to strengthen your core and your lower back (and so ward off back problems), as well as boost circulation – a fairly straightforward posture to help improve fitness and strength.

1. **Kneel on your mat**, making sure that your knees are hip-width apart, back is straight and tummy muscles relaxed but firm.

2. **Step forwards** with your left foot, placing it around one metre in front of your left hip. Your left thigh should be parallel to the floor, and your back should be straight. Imagine a line running directly from your left knee to your left heel.

3. **Flex your right foot** so that your lower leg is extended backwards from the knee. Maintaining an upright posture, bend forwards through your left knee. This will help to increase the stretch of your hips and hamstrings.

bottom tucked under – don't be tempted to arch your back.

6. **Fix your gaze** on a spot in front of you. Hold this pose for several breaths.

7. **Return to starting position** and repeat on the opposite side.

4. **Lift your arms**, so that your palms meet over your head. Hook your thumbs together. This should create an instant opposing pressure between your hands.

5. **Move into a lunge**, by slightly raising your back knee. Keep your

Frog Pose (Bhekasana)

A difficult pose, which challenges your boundaries, both emotionally and physically. As you practise yoga more and more, you'll find that your mind will begin to open and, simultaneously, so will your muscles and body.

1. **Lie face down** on the mat.

2. **Bend the knees** by bringing your feet towards your bottom and place the hands on the top of your feet.

3. **For beginners**, it may be advised to do this one leg at a time.

4. **Exhale**, and lift the head, chest and shoulders.

5. **Press the tops** of your feet down. Your feet should be grazing the side of your bottom or hips. If you can, turn your hands, so that your fingers match the direction of your toes.

6. **Hold the pose** for 20 to 60 seconds. Release slowly, preferably one leg at a time.

Top Tip

By opening your hip area, you'll strengthen your lower back, improve your digestion and improve the detoxification of your system.

Camel Pose (Ustrasana)

A good pose for those who jog or don't stretch correctly, as it gently works the thighs, shins, calves and pelvis. If your knees or shins hurt, place a blanket under them for extra support.

1. **Kneel** on your mat, keeping your knees hip-width apart. Prepare for the move by concentrating on pressing your shins and the tops of your feet into the floor.

2. **Place each hand** onto each buttock, spreading your palms and fingers over the entire area, fingers facing down. Lightly press your fingers against your bottom, pushing it slightly forwards, while keeping your thighs still. If you can't reach back this far, place them on your hips.

Top Tip

As this is quite a tough stretch, it's a good idea to return to Child Pose (page 89) for a few minutes afterwards to rest your body.

3. **Open your shoulder blades** up by breathing in and pulling them slightly down and across your back. Your upper torso is now upright, with a slight lean to the back.

4. **Lean slightly backwards**, so that your pelvis tilts – very slightly – forwards. Your hands should still be on your bottom, which will help you tilt the pelvis.

5. **If you're just starting out**, twist your torso slightly to the right so that you can reach your right foot. Then repeat with the left side. Don't worry if you can't

reach your feet on your first few tries; bring your feet to rest on your toes to lessen the distance to your heels.

6. **Keep your torso strong**, but soft. Make sure that you haven't tightened your stomach muscles, and your pelvis and chest aren't rising upwards.

7. **Breathe in**, then, on the exhalation, stretch through your arms, imagining that your ribs are lifting up and away from your pelvis. The insides of your elbows should be facing into your body. Increase the stretch by opening out your hands, and feel the extension through your upper body, right through to your fingers.

8. **Keep your head neutral**, so your gaze is fixed upon the ceiling. Make sure that your throat isn't tight and constricted. If it is, reduce your stretch.

9. **Hold** this pose for 30 seconds, building up to one minute.

10. **To return** to neutral, breathe in, then, on the exhalation, place your hands on your hips or pelvis, fingers pointing downwards. Squat your hips slightly downwards, returning your head and upper body upright.

East Stretch Pose (Purvottanasana)

A reverse of the downward Plank Pose (page 122), this stretch opens your chest area and counteracts the stretch from the plank. So, it makes sense not to do one without the other.

1. **Begin in Seated Staff Pose** (page 91), and place your hands behind your hips, fingers pointing towards your body.

2. **Bend your knees**, with your feet firmly on the mat around 30 centimetres away from your bottom. Turn your big toes slightly inwards.

Caution

Don't bend your back when you're lifting your leg, otherwise you'll find that your lower back will hurt the next day, or worse, straight away.

1

4. **Remain steady**, and straighten your legs, left leg first, then right leg. Your bottom muscles shouldn't be engaged – use your leg muscles and abdominals to lift. Feel your shoulder blades slide open and down your spine.

5. **Gently lift your head** slightly upwards. If you have neck problems, keep your head parallel to the floor.

6. **Hold** this pose for 30 seconds. Return to Seated Staff Pose.

3. **On the out breath**, lift your hips until they are parallel with the floor, so that your tummy forms a table. Your upper body and thighs should be parallel to the floor.

Bridge Pose (Setu Bandhasana)

The picture tells the story. The Bridge Pose improves the flexibility and strength of your spine. Remember to support your lower back with your hands; don't place them on your hips.

1. **Lie on your mat** with your feet about 50 centimetres apart, knees bent, feet flat on the floor. If you have neck problems, place a thickly folded blanket under your shoulders.

2. **Take a few breaths** to relax your neck and shoulders. Your arms should be relaxed beside your torso.

3. **Breathe out**, and push firmly through your feet and arms, to help push your torso upwards. Imagine that your tailbone is propelling your pubic bone upwards.

Top Tip

This is a great pose if you're feeling tired, or your mood is low. If you've been on your feet all day, perform this when you get home to relieve aching legs.

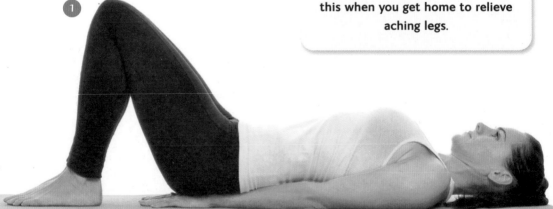

4. **Check your shoulders**. Reach down to clasp your hands on the floor under your pelvis. This will help lift you up onto your shoulders.

5. **Lift your buttocks**, keeping your knees directly over the heels. To ensure your body doesn't rock, push through your knees, away from your belly button.

6. **Hold** this position for 30 seconds to one minute, breathing slowly and deeply.

7. **To return to the start**, roll your spine gently down the mat until your back is flat on the floor.

Top Tip

If you have menstruation pains, put a pillow or folded blanket under your back to relieve lower-back pain.

Fish Pose (Matsyasana)

This pose is thought to be the 'destroyer of all diseases'. It stretches your entire body and gives your internal organs a good workout too.

1. **Lie** on your back, knees bent, feet firmly planted on the floor, arms close to your sides.

2. **Inhale and lift** your pelvis very slightly off the floor. You should feel a lovely loosening in your lower back.

3. **Place your hands**, palms down, under your bottom. Your bottom should now be resting on the backs of your hands. Keep your elbows close to your sides, so you can feel their pressure.

4. **Breathe in**. Firmly press your forearms and elbows into the floor and lift your upper torso and head off the floor.

5. **Tilt your head** slightly backwards so that the top of your head is as close as possible to the floor. If you can only rest the back of your head due to stiffness or neck and back problems, don't worry.

Top Tip

If your neck hurts in this pose, place a thickly folded blanket under it for support during the final steps.

3

6. **Check your thighs**, and make sure that they are flat on the floor, thighs strong and feet pushing forwards.

7. **Continue** with your breathing and remain here for 15 to 30 seconds. If you feel any crunching or pain in your neck, slowly return to neutral.

Reclining Hero Pose (Supta Virasana)

If you run or spend hours at your desk, your thigh muscles may be tight. To counteract any stiffness, do this pose after exercising. However, if you feel pain in the knees, place a folded blanket under them or only stretch as far as you can without discomfort.

1. **Begin in Hero Pose** (page 99), with your knees bent, feet slightly apart with your bottom between them.

2. **Exhale**, and slowly lower yourself backwards to the mat, focusing on your lower back first, as though you're unfurling. To help make this move easier, place your hands behind you and, as you lower yourself, rest on your forearms and then your elbows. This should help relieve any pain in your lower back and hips.

Top Tip

If you're menstruating or have PMS, this move will help relieve tired, aching legs, digestion and other related symptoms.

3. **Once you're leaning on your elbows**, place your hands under your buttocks and, as you slightly lift your pelvis off the floor, spread your buttocks evenly to the tailbone.

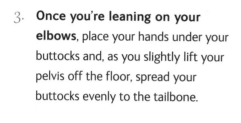

4. **Continue to lift** your pubis from the floor; this will help to release a tight groin. If this move is difficult, place a bolster or folded blanket under your shoulders for support.

5. **If you feel pain** or tightness in your knees, come out of this pose, as this stretch isn't intended to be felt there.

6. **Hold** this pose for 30 seconds, over time increasing the hold to five minutes.

7. **Return to the starting position**, using your elbows and forearms to push against the floor. Use your hands to lift your upper body into a sitting position.

Wheel Pose (Chakrasana)

It sounds incredible, but during this pose you'll stretch your body so far that it will actually begin to resemble a wheel. As well as an intense stretch, this posture is an all-over massage for your back, spinal column, arms, wrists and legs.

1. **Lie flat on your back** on your mat. Bend your knees and place your feet about 30 centimetres apart, as close to your bottom as you can.

2. **Bend your elbows**, and place your palms on either side of your head, just near your ears. Your fingers should be pointing in towards your shoulders.

3. **Press your feet firmly into the floor** and, as you breathe out, push yourself up, using your pelvis as the centre guide, until your thighs are parallel to the floor. Don't tighten your buttock muscles;

Top Tip

If you suffer from respiratory problems or asthma, try this pose to help clear your airways.

you should be using your pelvis and abdominal muscles to do this move.

4. **Continue to push** yourself up, pressing firmly through your palms, keeping your neck and head soft. As you push further, your head will drop back, so that you can see behind you.

5. **For some people**, this may be as far as they can stretch. If so, remain in this position, breathing steadily, for up to 30 seconds.

6. **If you can stretch further**, exhale and lift your head higher off the mat by straightening your arms, and pushing your pelvis towards your belly button.

7. **Hold** for five to 10 seconds. Lower your body to the ground and repeat up to five times.

4

Arm Balances and Inverted Postures

Keeping your upper body strong, especially your arms, shoulders and wrists, is essential for keeping your skeletal structure in balance. Also building strength and balance, while delivering a host of physiological benefits, inverted poses can be a challenge, but one well worth the effort.

Why It's Important to Have Strong Arms

Toned and strong arms will help you not just in terms of increased upper-body strength, but they will propel you in other exercises. Strong arms and a solid upper body can also help maintain balance.

It can be difficult and tiring at first, and you may find that your wrists are weak or painful during a pose, or your arms wobble uncontrollably when you first start trying to bear your weight. Don't give up. You can use straps to firm up your stance, blankets or the wall as support, as you slowly become stronger and more flexible.

Turning Yoga On Its Head

The practice of inversions is said to positively influence the following major systems: cardiovascular, lymphatic, nervous and endocrine. When you're upside down, you give your heart a break from sending all that blood and oxygen to the rest of your body. Headstands, and other inverted poses, improve circulation, stimulate the brain, enhance the functioning of the glandular system, and relieve pressure on the abdominal organs. Inversions also improve the return of venous blood – the veins that return blood to the heart – as these veins can't push blood against the force of gravity on their own, but require the action of muscular forces to propel the blood back up to the heart.

Caution

Pregnant or menstruating women should not perform inverted poses.

Benefits of Inversions

We all know that exercising is good for the heart, but inversion exercises provide another set of benefits. When your body is upside down, the pull of gravity draws the blood from the legs and lower back, back to the heart. This increase of blood flow stretches the heart muscle, which then contracts more powerfully, pumping an increased amount of blood to the whole body.

You'll also think more clearly after performing inverted poses, because the brain receives an oxygen boost. If you perform these poses after a long day sitting, or when you're fatigued, or at times when you need to concentrate, you'll notice the difference.

Crane Pose (Bakasana)

Also known as Crow Pose, this move draws upon all your upper-body and abdominal strength, and gives an all-over stretch. Use blocks to lean on if your wrists hurt, or begin to ache.

1. **Stand** with your feet hip-width apart. Breathe in and lower your body into a squat. Your feet may automatically lift up from the mat – if you can't keep your heels on the floor, place a thickly folded blanket underneath them.

2. **Widen your knees** and lean forwards, between your thighs. Place your hands on the floor, or onto blocks if you can't reach, elbows bent. Your upper arms should be pressing against your inner thighs. Come onto tiptoes, ready to lift.

2

Top Tip

If you're just starting out, you may find that this pose is difficult or causes pain in your wrists. Make sure that your heels and hips are close together and your body is tucked in tight. This will make it easier to balance and get into the right position. Use your upper arms to press against your shins for support.

3. **Lift both legs**, so that your entire body weight is resting evenly on your palms. Keep your head lifted so that you're gazing straight ahead of you.

4. **Hold** for up to 30 seconds. Return your feet to the floor and slowly return to a standing position.

Caution

If you're pregnant, it's advised that you avoid this move.

3

Inclined Plane Pose (Vasisthasana)

This posture strengthens the wrists, arms, shoulders and abdomen, important for skeletal and core health. The last few steps also stretch and warm up the legs. Remember to keep your core strong.

1. **From Plank Pose** (page 122), where your body is off the mat, resting on your hands and feet, shift your weight onto your right arm as you roll onto the outside of your right foot.

2. **Move your body weight slightly forwards** to your right forearm. You should feel a shift in your balance as you lean to the right.

3. **Turn your torso** to the left as you reach your left hand towards the ceiling. You should feel your abdominal muscles 'turn on' as they keep your body strong.

4. **Turn your head** to look towards your left hand.

2

5. **Hold** this position for five to 10 breaths.

6. **If you can**, bring the left knee towards your chest. Grab hold of your big toe with the index and middle finger of your left hand.

7. **Straighten your leg** and stretch your left arm upwards.

8. **Turn your head** to face your big toe. Hold for five to 10 breaths.

9. **To return to neutral**, exhale, lower the raised leg, release the toe and replace the left hand, then the feet back to stretch for a few breaths in Downward-Facing Dog Pose.

10. **Repeat** on the other side.

One-Hand-Over-Arm Balance (Eka Hasta Bhujasana)

Also known as Elephant Trunk Pose, there's nothing small about this move. Create definition and tone in your legs, hamstrings and buttocks, as well as improving your arm and upper-body strength.

1. **Sit with your legs crossed**, shoulders slightly forward. Your spine should feel long and supple.

2. **Use your hands** to lift your right shin off the floor and straighten out your leg, using a block under your right foot if this helps. Keeping your right leg parallel to the floor, slide your left arm down until you're almost hugging your left shin.

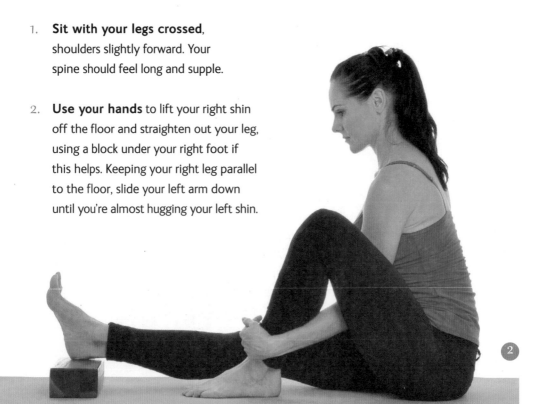

2

3. **Move your arm** until your left knee is nestled into the crook of your left elbow, or hold your right knee with your right hand and your left knee with your left hand.

4. **Warm your hip** and thigh area up, by gently rocking the right leg.

5. **Let go of your left knee**, and thread the left arm under the left knee, and place your left hand on the ground just outside the left buttock.

6. **Place your right hand on the floor** beside the right thigh. Check that your hands are parallel to each other.

7. **Inhale**, activating your abdominal muscles, your core and your left leg. Exhale, and press firmly into both palms and lift your bottom and left leg off the floor. The only part of your body now touching the floor should be your hands.

8. **Hold** for three to five breaths. Keep your right leg and foot flexed.

9. **Exhale**, and return to sitting.

10. **Return your left leg** to the starting position. Take some breaths here to recover and rejuvenate your energy.

Easy Inversion (Viparita Karani)

This shoulderstand is one of the easiest versions, so it's ideal for beginners. You'll need two thickly folded blankets or a bolster, and a wall for support.

1. **Sit** around 12 centimetres away from the wall, on the edge of your blanket or bolster (if you're right-handed, sit facing right, the opposite for left-handers).

2. **Breathe** out, and swing your legs up the wall, while simultaneously lying on the mat. Try to do this in one smooth movement, although it will take practice. Your bottom should be as close as possible to the wall.

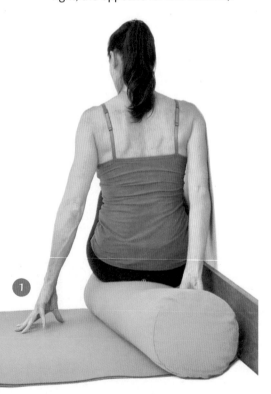

3. **There should be a slight arch** between your pubic bone and shoulders. If there isn't, bend your knees, press your feet firmly into the wall and lift your lower back slightly off your support and move the support downwards. Lower your lower body.

4. **Open your shoulder blades** away from the spine and release your hands and arms out to your sides, palms up.

5. **Your legs** should be firm enough to stay upwards against the wall, but not strong enough to engage your thighs.

6. **Lower** your gaze and allow your vision to soften.

7. **Hold** this pose for up to five minutes. As your mind and body relax, you'll become more and more comfortable. Add an eye mask, lavender-scented perhaps, to help you relax.

8. **To return to sitting**, allow your body to slide off your support and turn onto your side (the same side you began from). Remove the bolster from behind you and remain on your side, breathing in and out.

9. **Slowly** push yourself up to sitting.

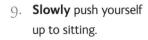

Benefits

This posture is ideal for tired or cramped legs and feet, or swollen ankles.

Hare Pose (Sasankasana)

A face-lift in a pose. The Hare Pose speeds up circulation to your face, so you'll look glowing and youthful after performing this. It also strengthens the pelvis, ribcage, back and arms. It provides an intense stretch to the back part of the body in the gluteals, arms, back, neck and shoulders.

1. **Kneel** on your mat with both palms placed on your knees or by your sides. Sit upright with your gaze straight ahead.

2. **Inhale**, and bring your hands directly above your shoulders.

Top Tip

This pose is recommended if you're feeling anxious, as it helps to regulate your breathing.

3. **Slowly exhale**, and reach down to touch the floor with your head and both your hands. Your fingers should be flexed outwards to cover as much space as possible. Relax when your forehead and palms touch the floor. Some areas of your chest and abdomen will rest on your thighs.

4. **Exhale**, and bring your palms to hug your knees.

5. **Repeat** five to seven times.

Plough (Halasana)

A very calming pose, this silences a busy mind and helps you leave stresses behind. It's also recommended for those going through the menopause, or if you're having a particularly bad PMT day.

1. **Lie flat** on your back, arms by your sides. Use a folded blanket to protect your elbows if you like. Bring your knees up.

2. **Slowly raise** your legs. Use your hands to push against the floor as you lift your lower back.

3. **Continue lifting** until your legs are bent over and beyond your head, as far back as possible. Once you have moved as far as comfortable, press your chin into the pit of your throat.

4. **Place your hands** on your lower back and support your back with elbows on the ground. Try touching the ground with your toes. Remain here for as long as you can, breathing normally.

5. **Slowly unroll** back into a lying position, pressing your hands against the floor to support your body weight.

Shoulderstand (Sarvangasana)

An all-over body stretch and stimulator, this pose may look daunting and it can take time to perfect. Don't be put off, as the benefits far outweigh the effort required.

1. **Lie flat** on your back, arms by your sides. Cushion yourself with a folded blanket if you like.

2. **Inhale,** and bend your legs at the knees and bring your knees towards your chest.

3. **Exhale** and lift your hips off the floor and place your hands against your lower back for support.

Top Tip

This is a perfect morning pose. This posture lifts and sustains your energy levels dramatically when practised every day.

2

4. **Lift** the rest of your body off the floor with the help of your hands (elbows staying on the floor for support).

5. **Extend** your legs upwards, towards the sky or ceiling. Imagine somebody is lifting your legs upwards towards the sky.

6. **Put as little pressure on** your head and neck as possible. Shoulders should be bearing the pressure, not the head and neck. Have your chin pointing towards your chest, in a 'chin lock' position. Never turn your head when you are in this position!

7. **Breathe**. Stay in this position for one minute. As you become stronger and more comfortable, remain here for five minutes. Any time you feel any type of discomfort, bend your knees towards your head and slowly roll your spine back to the ground.

6

Headstand (Sirsasana)

One of the 'ultimate' inversion postures, doing a headstand and holding it is the goal for many who practise yoga. Little wonder: performing this move helps to strengthen the immune system, stimulates the nervous system and improves the lungs and digestive system, among many other benefits.

1. **Start** by kneeling, facing a wall. Cross your arms so your elbows are lightly held by the opposite hand.

2. **Lean your upper body forwards** and rest your forearms on the floor.

3. **Without moving the elbows**, open the forearms into a triangular shape, creating an 80-degree angle. Interlace your fingers.

Top Tip

When you've completed this pose, rest in Child Pose (page 89) for at least 10 seconds.

4

4. **Place the crown of the head** on the floor, supported by the hands.

5. **Straighten your knees** and walk them closer towards your head.

6. **Lift your legs up**, balancing them against the wall to begin with, until you can balance holding your body upright. Bring both feet away from the wall, keeping your legs straight. Breathe normally and concentrate on your breath for balance. Reverse your steps slowly to return to the start.

Tripod Pose (Salamba Sirsasana)

While this position seems to defy gravity, it has numerous health advantages. Performing this move helps to strengthen the immune system, stimulates the nervous system and improves the lungs and digestive system, among many other benefits.

1. **Rest** on your mat in Child Pose (page 89). If you prefer, rest your head on a blanket.

2. **Kneel**, and place your hands flat on the floor, shoulder-width apart, with your elbows above your hands. Tuck your toes under.

3. **Inhale**, and straighten your knees.

4. **Walk your feet** towards your head.

5. **Now exhale**, and lift your feet off the floor; keep your thighs turned inwards slightly while doing this.

6. **Press** your tailbone firmly back against the base of your pelvis. Do not arch your back. Stretch your legs upwards.

7. **Hold** for 10 seconds or longer, depending on your comfort level.

8. **Return** to neutral by exhaling and ensure that both your feet touch the floor at the same time.

Checklist

Sitting and Floor Postures

- ☐ Corpse Pose
- ☐ Child Pose
- ☐ Seated Staff Pose
- ☐ Easy Seated Pose
- ☐ Lion Pose
- ☐ Head-To-Knee Pose
- ☐ Seated Forward Bend
- ☐ Hero Pose
- ☐ Heron Pose
- ☐ Gate Pose
- ☐ Seated-Angle Pose
- ☐ Seated Side Stretch
- ☐ Cobbler's Pose

Standing Postures

- ☐ Mountain Pose
- ☐ Tree Pose
- ☐ Chair Pose
- ☐ Triangle Pose
- ☐ Half-Moon Pose
- ☐ Warrior Poses
- ☐ Extended-Angle Pose
- ☐ Wide-Legged Forward Bend
- ☐ Standing Forward Bend
- ☐ Single-Leg Forward Bend
- ☐ Eagle Pose
- ☐ Dancer's Pose

☐ Reclining Bound-Angle Pose
☐ Garland Pose
☐ Cow-Face Pose
☐ Sage Pose
☐ Lotus Posture
☐ Downward-Facing Dog Pose
☐ Plank Pose
☐ Four-Limbed Staff Pose

Twists and Abdominal Toners
☐ Double Leg Raises
☐ Boat Pose
☐ Revolved Easy Pose
☐ Half Spinal Twist
☐ Revolved Abdomen Pose
☐ Pendant Pose

Back-Bending Postures
☐ Locust Pose
☐ Cobra Pose
☐ Upward-Facing Dog Pose
☐ Crocodile Pose
☐ Crescent-Moon Pose
☐ Frog Pose
☐ Camel Pose
☐ Easy Stretch Pose
☐ Bridge Pose
☐ Fish Pose

☐ Reclining Hero Pose
☐ Wheel Pose

Arm Balances and Inverted Postures
☐ Crane Pose
☐ Inclined Plane Pose
☐ One-Hand-Over-Arm Balance
☐ Easy Inversion
☐ Hare Pose
☐ Plough Pose
☐ Shoulderstand
☐ Headstand
☐ Tripod Pose

Developing Your Practice

Sequences of Asanas

Now that you've read through the asanas, and maybe even tried a few, it's time to put your knowledge into practice. One of the wonderful things about yoga is that you can pick and choose your poses, to fit in with your time schedule, ability, health, or emotional need. Ideally, don't begin a sequence with a difficult move. Instead, warm up slowly, with easier moves, which will encourage flexibility and blood flow to your limbs, allowing you to reach those harder stretches.

How To Design A Sequence

One asana you must always include in your yoga practice is your resting pose, or Corpse Pose (Savasana, page 88). Even if you only perform one pose after this, as long as you have given yourself the time and space to rest, breathe deeply and evenly, and relax your mind, you'll still feel the benefits of yoga.

A good way to decide which postures would suit you on a given day is to gauge your emotional and physical temperature. Are you feeling tired, in need of motivation, or do you need to unwind? Does your back hurt, or is your neck stiff? Is your period due? Taking the time to find out how you're feeling and what you need will give you a starting point from which to plan your sequence.

Where To Start

After your warm-up, you should ideally begin in a standing pose. This is because these poses help you to ground your energy while warming up your body. This in turn will help you remain strong throughout your session. After your body feels suitably warmed, move onto your chosen poses, each one followed by its counter pose. For instance, backward and forward bends are the usual counters of each other: after you complete a Cobra Pose (page 146), you could complete a forward bend, such as Child Pose. Some poses contain their own counterbalance, such as side-to-side stretches. You should also ensure that, if a pose requires you to move one side of the body in a move, you always repeat the move with the other side.

Finishing your sequence is ideally done by completing poses that involve lying on your mat. This final part of your sequence segues easily into Corpse Pose, where you can rest for as long as you need, or have time to.

Warm-Up Sequences

Launching yourself directly into your yoga moves may mean that your body and mind won't receive the full benefits of your poses. Your body and mind need some time to adjust to their new surroundings, as well as having to 'switch off' from a busy or stressful day. While stretching isn't necessary for sports such as running or swimming, performing warm-up exercises for your yoga session is as important as having the correct equipment.

Why You Should Warm Up

Warming up your body before you begin your poses or sequences maximizes blood flow to the muscles and makes the tendons more flexible. You'll find that you'll be able to reach further, and hold poses for longer without injury or pain.

Warming Up Your Emotions

Warming up your mind and emotions for a yoga session is also imperative, as it helps to create a separation from your busy day. During our usually hectic lives, it's not often that we take time to be still, to breathe and to calm our minds. Unfortunately, we can't just turn the channel off, or lower the volume of a busy mind. However, by calming your breathing and giving yourself the space to move in a safe, relaxing environment, you can adjust the dial on your mind.

Of course, each yoga pose, and sequence, will naturally warm up your body. The concept of a separate warm-up is to help both mind and body get into a 'yoga zone', as well as to reduce the chances of injury or strain.

When To Practise

A warm-up sequence such as Sun Salutation (page 196) can be performed at any time of the day but, as its name suggests, is best done in the morning. Although it is perfectly possible to perform it at the end of the day, you don't want to over-stimulate yourself. Rather, at the end of a busy day, focus on relaxation poses instead.

Sun Salutation Sequence (Surya Namaskar)

This pose pays respect and tribute to the sun, the source of energy. Ideally, perform in the morning, facing east, for an uplifting start to the day. There are many variations, but the following steps represent the most commonly practised sequence. Start slowly; over time, it will flow more naturally.

1. **Stand in Mountain Pose** (page 58). Inhale, and stretch your arms to the side and over your head, even with your ears. Breathe out, and bend into...

2. **Standing Forward Bend** (page 79). Breathe in, and lift your torso away from your legs. Your head should be lifted, eyes facing straight ahead. Exhale, and step back into...

3. **Plank Pose** (page 122). Breathe in, and feel the stretch in your spine. Breathe out, and move into...

4. **Four-Limbed Staff Pose** (page 124). If this is too difficult, rest your knees on the floor. Inhale, and push forwards into...

5. **Upward-Facing Dog Pose** (page 147). Exhale, and plant your feet firmly on the mat. Push your body into...

6. **Downward-Facing Dog Pose** (page 120). Breathe deeply for five breaths.

7. **On your fifth breath out**, bend your knees, inhale and step your feet between your hands. Return to...

8. **Standing Forward Bend**. Inhale, and slowly bring yourself to standing, drawing your arms back up over your head.

9. **Return to Mountain Pose**. Repeat the entire sequence as many times as you can.

Beginner Sequences

We all have to start somewhere. This gentle, easy-to-follow sequence is ideal for those at the start of their yoga journey. Each pose is easy to hold and, so you shouldn't be discouraged. As always, stretch only as far as you comfortably can and use the corpse pose to rest and recover between poses.

15-Minute Beginner Sequence

1. **Deep abdominal breathing** – one minute (page 223)

2. **Lie in Corpse Pose** (page 88), palms resting on your abdomen, fingers loosely spread apart. As you breathe slowly and steadily, feel the movement between your first rib, belly button and hips

3. **Sun Salutation** (page 196) – repeat four times

4. **Corpse Pose** – hold for eight breaths

5. **Head-to-Knee Pose** (page 94) – four each side

6. **Corpse Pose** – hold for eight breaths

7. **Shoulderstand** (page 182) – hold for one minute

8. **Corpse Pose** – hold for eight breaths

9. **Plough Pose** (page 180) – one minute

10. **Corpse Pose** – hold for eight breaths

11. **Fish Pose** (page 162) – hold for 30 seconds

12. **Boat Pose** (page 130) – hold for 30 seconds. Repeat.

13. **Final relaxation** – choose between Corpse Pose and Child Pose (page 89). Maintain your relaxation pose for up to six minutes

30-Minute Beginner Sequence

As you become used to the previous sequence, or find that you're able to make more time for your daily yoga routine, you can move on to this slightly more difficult routine. The moves should take you around 30 minutes and you can choose up to 10 minutes of relaxation at the end.

1. **Deep abdominal breathing** – one minute (page 223)

2. **Full yogic breath** – 10 breaths (page 223)

3. **Skull Shining (Kapalabhati) breathing** (page 226) – two rounds

4. **Corpse Pose** – hold for eight breaths

5. **Sun Salutation** – repeat four times

6. **Corpse Pose** – hold for eight breaths

7. **Single-Leg Forward Bend** (page 81) – repeat six times on each leg

8. **Corpse Pose** – hold for eight breaths

9. **Shoulderstand** – hold for one minute

10. **Corpse Pose** – hold for eight breaths

11. **Fish Pose** – hold for one minute

12. **Corpse Pose** – hold for eight breaths

13. **Boat Pose** – repeat twice

14. **Corpse Pose** – hold for eight breaths

15. **Single-Leg Forward Bend** – hold for 30 seconds on each leg

16. **Corpse Pose** – hold for eight breaths

17. **Inclined Plane Pose** (page 172) – hold for 30 seconds

18. **Corpse Pose** – hold for eight breaths

19. **Camel Pose** (page 155) – hold for up to 30 seconds

20. **Child Pose** – hold for eight breaths

21. **Triangle Pose** (page 65) – hold for 20 seconds on each side

22. **Final relaxation of Corpse Pose** – hold for up to 10 minutes, or longer as needed

Top Tip

If you experience any
pain, breathe in and
out and pull back
slightly on your stretch.

Intermediate Sequences

The following sequences are intended for those who have been practising yoga for some months, and can segue easily from one pose to the next. As always, pull back from a move if it's painful. If you can't hold a pose for the recommended time, then hold it for as long as you can and gradually, over subsequent sessions, build up the time you can hold the pose. Remember, you can return to a rest pose (Child Pose or Corpse Pose) whenever you need to.

Morning Routine

Start the day the right way with an uplifting and energizing sequence, designed to align your mind and body, boost your circulation and give you energy to face your day. This sequence should take you 20–30 minutes.

1. **Deep abdominal breathing** – one minute (page 223)

2. **Skull Shining (Kapalabhati) breathing** (page 226) – one round

3. **Sun Salutation** (page 196) – repeat five times

4. **Corpse Pose** (page 88) – hold for eight breaths

5. **Headstand** (page 184) – hold for one minute

6. **Child Pose** (page 89) – hold for eight breaths

7. **Fish Pose** (page 162) – hold for 30 seconds to one minute

8. **Boat Pose** (page 130) – repeat two to four times

9. **Corpse Pose** – hold for eight breaths

10. **Seated Forward Bend** (page 97) – hold for 30 seconds to one minute

11. **Inclined Plane Pose** (page 172) – hold for 15 seconds; repeat two to four times

12. **Half Spinal Twist** (page 134) – hold for 30 seconds on each side

13. **Final relaxation** – choose between Child Pose, Corpse Pose and lying on your mat, head turned to one side. Maintain your relaxation pose for up to six minutes

Evening Routine

This sequence should take you around 40 minutes. It's designed to help you stretch your body, wind down your mind and get your blood flowing (before calming it down) to remove the stresses and strains of the day. You can increase your relaxation time as needed when you've finished the sequence.

1. **Skull Shining (Kapalabhati) breathing** – one round

2. **Alternate Nostril (Anuloma Viloma) breathing**, page 225) – four rounds. Inhale for five seconds, hold for 20 seconds, and slowly exhale for 10 seconds. (Begin slowly. Try 5 in, 10 hold, 5 out to begin and work your way up.)

3. **Corpse Pose** – hold for eight breaths

4. **Sun Salutation** – repeat up to six times

5. **Corpse Pose** – hold for eight breaths

6. **Single-Leg Forward Bend** (page 81) – hold for 30 seconds and repeat on the other leg

7. **Corpse Pose** – hold for eight breaths

8. **Inclined Plane Pose** – hold for one minute

9. **Corpse Pose** – hold for eight breaths

10. **Headstand** – hold for up to one minute

11. **Corpse Pose** – hold for eight breaths

12. **Shoulderstand** (page 182) – hold for up to one minute

13. **Plough Pose** (page 180) – hold for up to one minute

14. **Fish Pose** – hold for 30 seconds

15. **Corpse Pose** – hold for eight breaths

16. **Wide-Leg Forward Bend** (page 76) – hold for one minute

17. **Seated Forward Bend** – hold for one minute

18. **Inclined Plane Pose** – hold for up to two minutes

19. **Corpse Pose** – hold for eight breaths

20. **Crescent-Moon Pose** (page 151) – hold for up to one minute

21. **Triangle Pose** (page 65) – hold for one minute

21. **Final relaxation of Corpse Pose** – hold for up to 10 minutes, or longer as needed

Closing Sequence

At the end of your session or sequences, your body and mind should be rewarded with a relaxation pose. This can be held for as long as you need. For beginners, it may be difficult to lie there and 'do nothing', even though this is the most important part of your session. The final relaxation pose will help your breath slow slightly. Your mind should drift, but don't worry if lots of thoughts race through your mind, just let them be. Slowly, your mind and body will relax into peacefulness.

Prepare To Relax

As you finish your relaxation sequence, your heart rate will drop, your body temperature will return to normal and your mind should be quietened. To aid your complete relaxation, you may need a yoga mat and, depending on the weather and room temperature or personal choice, a blanket (or even two).

1. **Lie on your back** in Corpse Pose. Your arms should be loose at your sides, legs slightly apart, feet slightly turned outwards. Take some deep abdominal breaths to centre yourself in this pose.

    You should be able to feel your body 'sink' into the floor.

2. **Inhale** and lift your right leg 10 centimetres off the floor. Make sure

your hips are still and your stomach muscles aren't engaged. You shouldn't feel the strain in your neck either.

3. **Hold this pose** for five seconds, then return to starting position. Repeat with the left leg.

4. **Inhale** and lift both arms 10 centimetres off the floor. Slightly tense your arms (but not your neck or shoulders) and allow your arms to slowly lower onto the mat.

5. **Breathe in**, and slightly lift your hips and buttocks off the floor. Hold for five breaths, and then return to the floor. You should tense your buttocks on the way down.

6. **Open your chest**. Inhale, and lift your chest off the mat. Don't lift too high, or your shoulder muscles will lift up towards your ears. Maintain a distance between your chin and chest area, by imagining that you're holding an orange beneath your chin. Hold for a few seconds, tense your shoulder blades by pulling them down your back, then exhale, and lower your upper body to the mat.

7. **Inhale** and lift your shoulders up towards your ears. Make sure that you're not pinching neck or shoulder muscles. If your neck or shoulders hurt, lower your shoulders slightly. Exhale, and return your shoulders to the starting position.

8. **Inhale** and scrunch up your face, so that you can feel all the muscles working. Hold your breath in this pose for the count of five, then exhale and release. This is a great way to reduce a tension headache or smooth out frown lines.

9. **Breathe in**, open your mouth wide, and stick your tongue out. Raise your eyes towards your eyebrows. You should feel your forehead wrinkling slightly and your eyebrows rising towards your hairline. Hold this pose for a count of five, then exhale, and return to rest.

10. **Inhale** and slowly turn your head to your right, keeping your chin slightly tucked under. Either look towards your right, or close your eyes. Hold for a few seconds and exhale, before returning to neutral. Repeat on the other side.

Struggling with Yoga

We all know that Rome wasn't built in a day. Neither was a handstand achieved in one yoga session. It's easy to compare yourself to others during a class, and become disillusioned that everybody else can achieve a full stretch, touch their toes, or perform a headstand without toppling over. It can feel even more demoralizing if your yoga neighbour is a couple of decades or more older than yourself!

A Mantra To Remember

Try to remember: yoga isn't a race. Nobody gets a gold medal just because they can reach a little further forwards than everybody else. Nobody wins a prize because they're able to move seamlessly into position without huffing and puffing or having to readjust limbs.

A good mantra to repeat whenever you're feeling that you compare unfavourably to others (or your own standards) is this: 'Where I am right now is exactly where I need to be.' Go on. Say it now. Now say it again. Can you feel your heart open a little and your mind relax? Even just the smallest amount?

Why Yoga Is All About You

We are raised to compete and compare. From birth, our parents compared our progress against other children's. We may have had to vie with siblings. Then we carried on competing through school with where we ranked in exam results; and on into adulthood with the size of our bank balances, houses, or cars. You know how it goes. Yoga is about stopping this way of thinking.

'Where I am right now is exactly where I need to be.'

In a yoga class, your individual insecurities or emotional issues can rise to the surface. So if you feel inferior, or lack confidence outside of the yoga room, it's very likely that you'll experience similar feelings when you're unable to complete a pose, or have difficulty reaching as far as you'd like. It's not unusual for tears to flow, your breath to speed up, and for you to feel an urgent need to leave the class. However, before you pack up your mat, try saying to yourself: 'Where I am right now is exactly where I need to be.' You'll find that your breath will slow, and those negative thoughts will recede.

Smile Through The Pain

Another great trick is to smile. If you can't reach that pose, then smile! If you fall over, smile! Seeing the humour in any situation allows you to take yourself and your practice less seriously. Remember, yoga is meant to bring light, energy and peace to your life, not stress and frustration.

Of course, if you feel physical pain or strain, then stop immediately. Ask your instructor for help and assistance. Pain on a movement usually occurs because it isn't being performed correctly, or you're trying to push yourself before your body is ready. Your instructor can show you an easier pose, or just how far you should go at that point in time.

Next time you feel frustrated or stressed during a class, stop, smile and say, 'Where I am right now is exactly where I need to be.'

Yoga For Health

As you have read throughout this book, certain poses are ideal for certain ailments or illnesses. We've collated the commonest health issues and suggested poses to try to help improve your health concerns – whether emotional or physical in origin.

To De-Stress

If you're stuck at your desk, but feel like you're about to explode, take some time to perform this de-stressing neck roll.

1. **Close** your eyes.

2. **Let your chin drop** onto your chest.

3. **Slowly begin** to move your neck and head in a circular motion by moving the right ear to the right shoulder, taking the head backwards and then bringing the left ear to the left shoulder.

4. **Keep your shoulders** loose and relax.

5. **Rotate** your neck in this way three to five times, and then switch directions.

De-Stressing Postures

- **Mountain Pose (page 58)**
- **Downward-Facing Dog Pose (page 120)**
- **Child Pose (page 89)**
- **Upward-Facing Dog Pose (page 147)**
- **Four-Limbed Staff Pose (page 124)**
- **Corpse Pose (page 88)**

Strength-Building Postures

- Upward-Facing Dog Pose
- Downward-Facing Dog Pose
- Seated Forward Bend (page 97)
- Bridge Pose (page 160)
- Revolved Easy Pose (page 132)
- Plank Pose (page 122)
- Half-Moon Pose (page 67)
- Crane Pose (page 170)

To Energize Body And Mind

- Downward-Facing Dog Pose
- Four-Limbed Staff Pose
- Cobra Pose
- Bridge Pose
- Fish Pose (page 162)
- Plank Pose (page 122)
- Shoulderstand (page 182)

To Kick-Start Weight Loss

- Seated Forward Bend
- Bridge Pose
- Chair Pose (page 63)

To Increase Confidence

- Mountain Pose
- Plank Pose
- Downward-Facing Dog Pose
- Tree Pose (page 60)
- Warrior Pose (page 69 or 71)

To Alleviate Back Pain

- Cobra Pose (page 146)
- Locust Pose (page 144)
- Dancer's Pose (page 84)
- Triangle Pose (page 65)
- Cow-Face Pose (page 115)

To Beat Premenstrual Syndrome Or Pain

- ✓ Bridge Pose
- ✓ Alternate nostril breathing (page 225)
- ✓ Dancer's Pose (page 84)
- ✓ Reclining Bound-Angle Pose (page 111)
- ✓ Child Pose (page 89)

To Beat Insomnia

- ✓ Meditation
- ✓ Corpse Pose

- ✓ Seated Forward Bend
- ✓ Seated-Angle Pose (page 105)
- ✓ Head-To-Knee Pose (page 94)

To Aid Conception And Fertility

- ✓ Bridge Pose (supported)
- ✓ Four-Limbed Staff Pose
- ✓ Reclining Bound-Angle Pose
- ✓ Head-To-Knee Pose
- ✓ Seated Forward Bend
- ✓ Shoulderstand (supported)
- ✓ Headstand (supported) (page 184)
- ✓ Easy Inversion (page 176)
- ✓ Wide-Legged Forward Bend (page 76)
- ✓ Garland Pose (page 113)
- ✓ Reclining Hero Pose (page 164)

To Reduce Eye Strain

Rub your hands together, until you feel the warmth between your palms. Gently place your hands over your closed eyes. Hold for 30 seconds.

Special Considerations

Although yoga is perfect for many ailments, there are some positions that may exacerbate certain health issues or that may be best avoided at certain times.

During Your Period

Yoga teachers and experts are divided on whether certain moves may be unwise for menstruating women to perform. It's believed that some poses – namely inversion poses – direct energy the wrong way, which can be detrimental during the menses. Also, as many women suffer from back and abdominal pain during this time, or before, extra pressure in these areas may exacerbate the issue. However, there are still many poses you can perform, some of which are in fact highly recommended, during your period. As women can suffer from many and various menstrual symptoms, such as irritability, bloating, tiredness, cramps and insomnia, yoga can help ease these. One of the main PMS complaints – irritability, leading to anger or tears – can be soothed with some gentle yoga moves and relaxation.

To Avoid During Your Period

- Headstand
- Shoulderstand
- Standing Forward Bend
- Downward-Facing Dog

During Pregnancy

Yoga is highly recommended during pregnancy, as it's believed to help keep joints supple, ease backache and may even lead to an easier birth. A recent study from the University of Michigan found that women who practised yoga during pregnancy were less likely to suffer from hormone-related depression and even reported a stronger bond with their baby. The researchers also found that regular yoga classes helped give pregnant women more energy and reduced overall stress levels. As with menstruation, there are some poses that aren't suitable for pregnant women – and those trying to conceive – and these are highlighted throughout the book. These include back bends, poses that require you to lie on your back (during the first trimester of your pregnancy), or ones that stress the abdominal muscles. This is because during pregnancy your body is flooded with the hormone relaxin, which helps the uterus expand, but softens the connective tissue, and this may lead to sprains or injuries. If you're attending yoga classes, make sure you tell your instructor you're pregnant. There are many yoga classes specially geared towards pregnancy, so you may want to try one of these instead.

To Avoid During Pregnancy

- **Back bends**
- **Balancing poses on one leg** **(unless supported by chair or wall)**
- **Headstand**
- **Shoulderstand**
- **Camel Pose**

Back And Neck Pain

While yoga is an excellent way to help heal a sore back or stiff neck, the poses must be conducted with care, to avoid further injury or strain. The most important thing to remember when performing a posture is to engage your abdominal muscles. These help reduce lower-back pain and stabilize the spine, thus reducing the chance of injury. The main reason back pain may occur after a yoga class is if you've performed the move incorrectly, or pushed yourself too far too soon. Remember that yoga isn't a race. It's all about you, your body and how you listen to its limitations and needs.

To Avoid If You Have Back Pain

- **Camel Pose**
- **Standing Forward Bend**
- **Cobra Pose**
- **Warrior Pose I**
- **Triangle Pose**
- **Wheel Pose**
- **Fish Pose**

Checklist

☐ **Build a sequence to suit**: You can pick and choose your postures, being sure to include counter postures – forward and backward bends – to suit your individual needs.

☐ **Your 'go to' pose**: Any sequence should include Corpse Pose (page 88), for maximum relaxation and to give your body a chance to absorb the effects of your other postures.

☐ **What a way to start the day**: Performing a Sun Salutation in the morning, facing east, will energize you and give you an uplifting start to the day.

☐ **And to end the day**: Yoga can be performed at any time, but, as many postures can be energizing, concentrate on relaxation poses or meditation in the evening.

☐ **So much to choose from**: There are literally hundreds of postures, all conferring health benefits. See our lists on pages 210–12 to help you decide which best suit your needs.

☐ **Always remember**: Your yoga practice is personal to you. Try not to compare yourself to others who might have been practising for years. Keep in mind: 'Where I am right now is exactly where I need to be.'

☐ **Remember to smile**: There's a perception among some that yoga must be taken terribly seriously. It is a discipline but one that's designed to help you think and feel better.

☐ **Listen to your body**: If you can't smile through the pain and you feel a real twinge or uncomfortable stretch, ease off immediately.

Breath Control

Pranayama

Pranayama is, in essence, the art of controlling the breath. The word comes from the Sanskrit meaning 'extension of the prana', the breath or life force. This concept is very important in yoga and is reflected in the prominence of pranayama. In fact, it is so important that many maintain that you are only doing yoga properly when you are breathing fully, consciously and correctly. Breathing is as fundamental to yoga as it is to life itself.

Breath of Life

Understanding pranayama is central to a long-term yoga practice. Those who can control their breathing are able to influence the mind and body in any number of ways. Properly performed breathing exercises can promote mental and physical wellbeing, making you calmer, more

peaceful, or reenergized and revitalized. Breathing is a direct link between you, your body and the outside world. Pranayama techniques can also be used for general stress relief and relaxation.

Breathing ABC

Contrary to common perceptions, there are actually more than two stages (inhaling and exhaling) to the breathing process. Remember, the respiratory system stretches all the way from the nose down to your lungs. In the yoga world, pranayama is so important that each and every step is carefully scrutinized. In actuality, there are four parts to the breath, which includes the points after exhalation and before inhalation, as well as breath retention.

- **Inhalation (puraka):** The first stage in the breathing process is the inhalation, which draws fresh air into the lungs, bringing vital new life-force energy, or prana, into your body.

- **Breath retention (kumbhaka):** After inhalation, this phase is the retention of the air in the lungs, prior to exhalation. In pranayama, breath retention should be effortless and natural, never strained or difficult, as if you were holding your breath.

- **Exhalation (rechaka):** The third stage is the exhalation and the expulsion of the air out of the body. Like the inhalation, this should typically be a smooth, continuous and relaxing process.

- **Pause after exhaling (kumbhaka):** The fourth stage is the pause after exhalation. This pause marks the end of the breath cycle, ahead of a new inhalation.

Incorporate Into Your Practice

If you can understand the significance of pranayama, and are able to perfect a few simple breathing techniques, this really is a tool you can take with you anywhere, helping you find inner calm, stress relief and relaxation wherever you go.

Did You Know?

If you thought you knew how to breathe, think again. Yoga takes breathing – an interaction with the universe itself – to an entirely new dimension.

The Benefits of Pranayama

Just watch your breath for a short while: sit comfortably, close your eyes and observe your breath gently come and go, rising and falling. The breath happens all by itself. By tuning in to this amazing natural phenomenon that we take for granted, we can start to appreciate the beauty and wonder of our own bodies, and of being alive. By drawing on prana, this abundant and free energy source, we can transform our health and well-being, boosting vitality, confidence and happiness.

A Host of Benefits

Pranayama presents an enormous range of benefits for both the mind and body. These include stress reduction and anxiety relief, through to improved sleep patterns and better concentration at work. Best of all, pranayama can be performed virtually anywhere, to give you a mind-body boost when and where you need it most. Breathing in this way, consciously and deliberately, focusing on something so small and yet so significant, is the simplest way to attain a greater sense of calm, relaxation and wellbeing.

Physical Benefits

By performing pranayama exercises on a regular basis, practitioners can start to feel direct physical benefits in their bodies. Slow, deep breaths are a quick

Top Tip

Simply by being still and watching your breath, in and out, for a period of time, is a fabulous way to find deep relaxation and calmness. Try it next time you find yourself under stress.

antidote to the common fight-or-flight response that generates stress in our bodies, which brings tension, aches and pains, and heightened anxiety levels. The knock-on effect can be physical ailments and headaches, or poor sleep patterns. Just some simple breathing exercises can make all the difference and, as well as relaxing your body, pranayama can help to restore your energy levels.

Emotional Benefits

Slow, conscious and deliberate breathing exercises can be an invaluable ally in the fight against stress. Pranayama is a great way for yogis (and non-yogis) to find deep relaxation and promote ongoing feelings of calmness and wellbeing, melting away the stresses of modern life. Breathing deeply in a conscious fashion can have a lasting impact in reducing anxiety levels, especially during difficult times, such as when sitting exams or other nerve-inducing situations. It also increases clarity of thinking and helps to combat a noisy or busy mind.

Learning To Breathe

Everyone can breathe, but yogis have got it down to a fine art. Most people don't realize they're not getting the best from their breath, taking shallow or hurried breaths, which may be the long-term effects of a less-than-optimum lifestyle, or possibly years of unmanaged stress. But it's never too late to learn to breathe.

Getting Started

A balanced rhythm of breathing means striking the balance between inhalation and exhalation, and the pauses in between. Pranayama exercises involve all of these component parts. Before you begin, it's good to take stock of what you've already got. Find a quiet place and tune in to your normal breathing at rest. Close your eyes, listen to and feel your breath. This will give you a marker, and let you monitor your progress as you proceed with new breathing techniques.

Any Time

For beginners, it's best to start small. Attend a basic yoga class, where pranayama is taught, and then practise the technique at home. Take a few minutes at first, rather than book in half an hour. The more time you spend, the more benefits you'll derive, but be realistic. Five minutes is better than none at all. Early in the morning is a good time to set you up for the day. In the evening, don't practise too close to bed time, as the exercises can be invigorating. Try not to practise on a full stomach.

Any Place

It doesn't really matter where you practise, just as long as you won't be interrupted. At home is good, as you can pack the kids off to school and switch off your mobile phone. Once you become more proficient, you'll be able to take pranayama anywhere you go. Finding peace through deep breathing during a busy day can be a blissful experience, and radically alter the outcome of the rest of the day. Best of all, go outside and find a park or garden where you can experience the life force all around you.

How To Sit

Many pranayama postures, especially those for the more experienced yogi, will require certain seated positions and mudras (hand gestures). For beginners, it's perfectly acceptable to find a comfortable seated position, preferably on the floor, though on a chair is fine if this is difficult. Some of the commonest asanas adopted during pranayama practice include Tailor Pose, Lotus Pose and Half Lotus Pose.

Top Tip

Weather permitting, head outdoors and breathe in the wonderful healing energy of nature all around. It's good for the soul.

Deep Abdominal Breathing and Full Yogic Breath

This is the basis for complete relaxation. First, in order to achieve deep abdominal breathing, you must fill your tummy with air – count to five on the in breath, and five on the out breath. Then move on to yogic breath, which incorporates inhaling through the abdomen first, followed by the chest: fill your abdomen, deep down, with your inhalation and continue inhaling, until your tummy is full and your chest rises with air. Exhale, emptying the chest area first (you'll be able to see it fall) and continue exhaling, as your tummy becomes concave. You've now completed one full round of yogic breath. Repeat for 20 rounds.

The Exercises

Try to remember that pranayama is so much more than breathing. Become more conscious of what you are doing. You are breathing with great awareness to invite the flow of prana, the force of life itself, deep into your whole being. There are many breathing exercises, some better known than others. Some may be found in beginner yoga groups, although others may be the preserve of more experienced practitioners. To fully learn and appreciate these techniques, it is always best to seek a trained instructor.

Bellows Breath (Bhastrika)

This is one of the most famous yogic breathing exercises. It's ideal if you're feeling sluggish and want to blow away the cobwebs. To get started, take a comfortable seated position. Take a few full breaths that go deep into your abdomen. When you're ready, after a strong inhalation, forcefully exhale through the nose, and then forcefully inhale through the nose. Each inhale and exhale should take just a second. In this exercise, your breathing is all done through the nose and from your diaphragm, so try to keep your head, shoulders and chest relatively still as your tummy moves. Take it easy at first if you're just starting out, and stop if you're feeling light-headed, as this is quite a powerful exercise. Don't do this one too close to bed time, as it is invigorating and may keep you awake.

Equal Breath (Sama Vritti)

This is a great exercise if you're looking to calm down or find a little peace. Take a comfortable seated position and close your eyes. At first, simply observe your breath as it is, your inhalation and exhalation, the rise and fall of the chest, and the various sensations as the air moves in and out through the nose. Then inhale slowly for the count of four, then do the same while you exhale. The inhalation and the exhalation should last for the same amount of time. You can continue this gentle breathing exercise for as long as you wish, or you might want to increase (or decrease) the number you count to as you breathe in and out.

Alternate Nostril Breathing (Anuloma Viloma)

This breathing exercise alternates between the nostrils. The right nostril breath links to the positive nadi (or 'energy channel' if you like), called Pingala, and activates the left side of the brain; the left nostril breath links to the mirroring nadi (Ida) and activates the right side of the brain. Sit comfortably. Inhale through the left nostril, closing the right nostril with your thumb. Hold briefly. Exhale through the right nostril, closing the left nostril with your index finger. Next, inhale through the right nostril, keeping the left one closed. Hold, then exhale through the left nostril, closing off the right. Repeat five times.

Skull Shining (Kapalabhati)

Great for bringing balance to your life and for detoxification, this rather forceful exercise may even give you a healthier, more vibrant glow (the Sanskrit phrase translates as 'shining forehead'). To get started, settle in a comfortable seated position. Breathe in deeply through the nose. As you exhale sharply through the nose, pull your stomach in, bringing your navel back towards your spine as much as you comfortably can. You can feel your abdominal muscles contract by placing your right hand on your stomach. Sustain this passive inhale and forceful exhale rhythm for about 20 breaths. Take a short break of normal breaths before starting again and performing another two rounds.

Cooling Breath (Shitali)

A breath to cool the body, this one is good if you're feeling over-heated or trying to contain anger. Sit comfortably, then stick out your tongue a little way, and curl the sides in and up, to form a tube. The end of the tongue is just outside the mouth. Inhale through the 'tube', feeling the cooling effect as you do so, then exhale through the nose. Repeat five times.

Hissing Breath (Sitkari)

This is another exercise that is good for cooling you down if you're feeling over-heated, or to help your focus. In this exercise, the breath makes a hissing sound, hence the name. Sit comfortably with a straight spine. With your mouth open, touch the hard ridge behind your teeth with your tongue. Then, if possible, close the top and bottom teeth together. Inhale through the mouth (and closed teeth) to make the hissing noise. Exhale immediately after, slowly and steadily, through the nose. Repeat up to five times.

Did You Know?

The flow of healing prana, or life-force energy, in and out of the body can induce a wonderful sense of calm, eat away stress, and send your spirits soaring.

Victorious Breath (Ujjayi)

This noisy breath, also known as 'ocean breath' (it creates an ocean-like sound), can have a relaxing effect on the body and can be useful for conditions such as insomnia. Commonly used in Vinyasa or more flowing styles of yoga, it can also have a warming or heating effect on the body, and may be useful for coughs and fevers. To begin, simply inhale and exhale through the mouth, deeply. Starting with the exhalation, begin to (very slightly) constrict the passage of air at the back of the throat. Then do the same on the inhalation (together, this should sound something like the ebb and flow of the ocean). Next, keeping the same

Top Tip

There are dozens of breathing exercises and all manner of variations of seating postures, hand gestures and mantras. Experiment with them, but, most importantly, find one that works for you.

breathing going, close the mouth and start to breathe through the nose instead; you should still hear the same loud breathing noise. Repeat five times, and work up to more after you have a little experience.

Humming Bee Breath (Brahmari)

Start this exercise in a comfortable seated position, with the body relaxed and the spine straight. Close your ears with your index fingers, and inhale through both nostrils. Then, start to create a humming sound as you exhale. The inhalation should be deep and strong, and the exhalation slow, steady and continuous, while the noise is made. After a while, you can also try the same with the inhalation, although this is a harder practice to master for newcomers.

Lion's Breath (Simhasana)

This is a great one for children, but for adults it can also be a good tension buster, stretching out the jaw and tongue during the forceful exhalation. To get the full lion effect, begin by kneeling, resting on your feet. Inhale through the nose. As you exhale, open the mouth wide, poke your tongue out and make a loud 'ha' sound, forcefully and very audibly. Return to a neutral expression as you inhale again. Repeat five times. For the detailed pose, see page 93.

Checklist

☐ **Calm down**: Pranayama exercises are an excellent way to foster a greater sense of peace and calm in your life. They can also be invigorating, uplifting and energizing.

☐ **Life force**: Pranayama is much more than simply breathing. It is about drawing life force and nature's raw energy directly into your body.

☐ **Four stages**: There are four parts to the breath: inhalation, breath retention, exhalation and the pause after exhaling. All of these stages are important.

☐ **Multiple benefits**: Better breathing can provide an all-round boost for your body, easing away tensions and stress, and improving your general health and wellbeing.

☐ **Breathe and go**: Once you have learned a few simple pranayama breathing techniques, you can perform them wherever you go, whenever you are in need of a lift.

☐ **Beginner's luck**: Some yoga traditions call for certain postures and mudras (hand gestures) during pranayama, but this is not always necessary when you're starting out.

☐ **Peace out**: Pranayama, rather like meditation, can be integrated into a broader relaxation or stress-reduction programme.

☐ **Take a break**: If ever you start to feel dizzy during any of the exercises, stop and take a break.

Meditation

Why Meditate?

The seventh step (or Dhyana) in the Eight Limbed yogic path, meditation is about cultivating a stillness of mind, training our attention inwards so we become more aware of ourselves and our place in the world and universe. Meditation has been proven to be a great comforter during times of intense emotional difficulty. The process is not so much about shutting out our thoughts (both positive and negative), but raising our ability to observe them, to then let them pass naturally and effortlessly.

Stress Free

Meditating is a great way to relax and unwind after work, or to help insulate yourself from the stresses of modern life. It's a simple practice, and many centuries old – people have been training their minds through meditation for thousands of years – but there's a lot of modern science to back it up. There are many types of meditation, but, in essence, it's simply training our attention inwards, to permit thoughts and any mental chatter to pass by, without struggle. People all over the world meditate to ease stress, relieve anxiety, or to improve their general health and wellbeing. This can result in a more balanced outlook on life, which, in turn, can make you feel happier, brighter, more alive, more in control.

Clear Thinking

We all know how much difference it can make at work or at home if you wake up with a clear head. You get more done, life seems just a little easier, you feel happier, more vibrant. Meditation can cut through all of the mental noise to create a healthier, internal mindset, which brings results in many other areas of your life. This includes improved feelings of inner balance, heightened creativity, flexibility and better decision-making. Your new-found emotional resilience means you are also more able to break bad habits, to manage any painful conditions. In general, you feel calmer and more able to cope with life.

Top Tip

Meditation is a great way to calm the mind and brush off stresses of work. Before a big meeting or presentation, take some quiet time to clear your mind and sharpen your thinking. You'll appreciate the extra clarity.

Key Benefits

These are just some of the other main benefits that a regular meditation practice can bring:

- Reduced stress
- Reduced anxiety
- Improved concentration
- Greater peace of mind
- Better emotional balance
- Lower blood pressure

Where To Start

The best thing about meditation is that you can perform it pretty much anywhere and at any time. If you're starting out, it can be helpful to consult an experienced meditation guide (your yoga teacher will be able to advise you). Many yoga classes may also include an introduction to meditation, and a group meditation can be a very powerful experience. For the most part, however, meditation is typically a solitary practice, performed in a quiet location, where you can be alone with your thoughts.

Set the Scene

You don't need any special place or equipment to meditate, but if you want to practise regularly, it can help to find a quiet spot you can go to each day. This will help you associate a place you know is safe and peaceful with your daily meditation fix. Needless to say, try to avoid distractions such as loud televisions or noisy children where possible.

Top Tip

The more you meditate, the more the benefits accrue, so try to incorporate it into your daily life as much as possible, whether that's at home, at work, or out and about.

Home Space

If you want to create a more conducive environment for your meditation at home, this can be easily achieved with some subdued lighting, soft music and soothing aromas. Playing some calming mantra music can help set the scene, or you might want to burn an incense stick.

When To Meditate

The most common prescription for regular daily meditation is to do it twice a day, with one session in the morning, shortly after waking, and one in the late afternoon or before you go up to bed (not in bed, as you may fall asleep). This may not always be possible, however, so it's important to be flexible in order to sustain your practice and not give up.

Keep It Real

Seasoned yogis and spiritual gurus can spend hours on end in just one meditation session. For most of us, however, it's important to keep it manageable. Just sitting for a couple of minutes at a time may be all that is required to start you off on the right track. The most important thing is to keep your practice going on a regular basis, as this is when the benefits will start to come. Look for meditation opportunities in your normal day: you could be sitting on the bus; you could switch off the television 10 minutes earlier; or you could take some time out to meditate during your lunch hour.

Choosing A Posture

How you sit whilst meditating is not so important. What you must ensure is that you are comfortable in order to give yourself the best chance of success, and that your posture allows you to remain alert and aware. There are some meditation styles that involve holding certain positions, or mudras (hand gestures), but most simply require you to sit, either on a chair or on the floor. Lying down is not recommended, as you may end up asleep – which is not meditation!

Where To Meditate

It doesn't really matter where you meditate. You can do it indoors or outside, moving on a train at 70 mph, or sitting cross-legged in the park. Your meditation experience will be different every time. The most important thing is that you are taking the time to journey within, to still the mind, and to tap into your inner consciousness. If you can find time and space at home to establish a regular meditation routine, all the better.

Top Tip

Meditation is for everyone, not just spiritual gurus. Try out a few different styles and find out what works best for you. Not all meditations are the same.

What To Wear

Likewise, it's not important what you wear, as long as you're comfortable and not constricted when you sit down. If you're at work, overalls or a pin-striped suit and bowler hat are equally good. Meditation is for everyone, so don't be put off by images of spiritual masters with long beards and floating robes.

Classic Postures

Here are some of the classic seated meditation postures that have been used by generations of yogis:

- **Full Lotus:** The classic cross-legged seated yoga position, this is where you cross your left foot over your right thigh and your right foot over your left thigh, alternating from time to time.

- **Half Lotus:** Similar to the Full Lotus but easier to execute, one foot is placed on the opposite thigh and the other foot on the floor beneath the opposite thigh.

- **Tailor Pose:** The simplest cross-legged position, with both knees on the ground, soles of the feet together.

- **Hero Pose:** This is a kneeling position where the buttocks rest either on the ground or on a block between your feet.

Hand Gestures

Some meditations require the use of mudras, or hand gestures, which carry special significance. Each mudra (there are dozens of them) has a meaning. The mudra is believed to enhance the meditation experience and to reinforce key messages.

Meditation Techniques

There are many different styles and types of meditation. Some focus on specific objects or sounds, or advanced breathing techniques, others involve holding more challenging physical positions. It can be helpful to explore this variety. Experience some of the options for yourself so you can find the one that suits you best. Personal preference is always the best gauge; no one technique is better than the other.

Types of Meditation

Given the wide range of benefits, it is little wonder that there are stacks of meditations out there, all with the goal of bringing you inner balance and harmony. None of these meditations is superior to any other, though some may be more popular, or more widely known, and others may have been around for longer. Typically, but not always, most meditations will start with some sort of breathing exercise, or observance. In all cases, the meditation experience is meant to invoke feelings of peace and calm, relaxation, clarity of thinking, vitality, a greater sense of perspective and renewed vigour.

Mindfulness Meditation

This popular form of meditation, which also encompasses many other types of meditation exercise, means being present in the here and now. The aim of this exercise is simply to pay attention, to be mindful, which in turn switches the mind's attention away from other distracting thoughts, such as events in the past or worries about the future. Mindfulness meditation is about simply being.

Top Tip

There is no right or wrong way to meditate, which is great news for beginners. It means you can never go wrong. You're taking time for yourself, to calm and balance your inner you. Go with the flow.

Breath Counting Meditation

Counting breaths can be a very effective way to quieten the mind for some people. It is also a good exercise for beginners, as there are no other spiritual or yogic connotations associated with it, plus it's very simple. Breaths are silently counted up to ten to prevent the mind from drifting too far, while focus and awareness is also centred on the actual process of breathing. If you lose count, then simply start again from one.

Body Scan Meditation

This form of meditation involves scanning through the whole body to still the mind and raise awareness of the physical condition. After observing the breath, the focus turns to one tip of the body, such as the left foot, and then proceeds through the body, from the tip of the toe to the top of the head. The focus on each single part of the body also brings a sense of rest to the mind, especially while concentrating on all of the different parts of the head.

Mantra Meditation

In this meditation, a sound or word or phrase is chanted and repeated either out loud or in silence. The mantra could be a modern word, such as a positive affirmation to encourage personal growth and development, or an ancient Sanskrit phrase. The mantra 'Om' is often used in yoga, as it delivers a powerful vibrational effect on the practitioner and all around. In this case, the sound and its vibration become the object focused on during the meditation.

Transcendental Meditation

This type of meditation involves quietening the mind through the use of a simple word repeated over and over again inside the head, in silence. Ideally practised for 20 minutes twice a day, it is a simple, natural and effortless procedure performed whilst sitting comfortably with eyes closed. Transcendental

meditation allows your mind to settle beyond your thoughts into the source of those thoughts, a place of pure awareness, also known as transcendental consciousness, or the unified field, where you can experience your innermost self.

Top Tip

You've always got time on your side. It's great if you can meditate for long periods, but just taking a couple of minutes of quiet time can really help to recharge your batteries.

Trataka Meditation

A simple but powerful exercise in concentration, *trataka* means 'to gaze steadily at a fixed point'. During this meditation, the practitioner gazes upon a small object (such as a candle flame or a tiny black dot, both of which are commonly used), tuning in to any thoughts and feelings as they arise, and then letting them go. After a time, the mind becomes completely absorbed in the object, to the point that it may be seen clearly when the eyes are eventually closed.

Top Tip

Don't think of meditation as a selfish pursuit. Sometimes it can help to think how the exercise will ultimately benefit those around you, if it is making you calmer, more refreshed, more balanced, with greater energy levels.

Candle Meditation

This is performed while gazing at a candle flame, similar in some ways to trataka meditation. It is a good choice for beginners, who may find it easier to let go of their thoughts whilst concentrating open-eyed on a flickering external flame, rather than tuning in to a mantra inside their head. The gentle flicker of the flame can lead to a deeply relaxed meditative state in a fairly short time, soothing mind chatter and bringing a deep sense of peace and wellbeing.

Guided Imagery Meditation

Also referred to as 'guided visualization', this meditation is popular with beginners for its simplicity and ability to engage the mind, leading it away from the usual thought processes. It involves listening to a guide as they take you through a series of relaxing visualizations. These 'inner journeys' can use very vivid imagery and can often be tailored to specific goals, such as helping you relax, or boosting confidence and self-esteem.

Five Senses Meditation

This meditation involves a brief relaxation before tapping into the five senses, through the sensory organs (eyes, ears, nose, tongue and skin). Meditating on these five senses can help to bring greater focus and awareness of sensory experience, enhancing your inner feelings of calm and vitality. The meditation usually involves observing and using all of the senses, one after the other, through a combination of exercises, such as recalling or picturing visual objects, or concentrating hard on a sound or smell.

Checklist

☐ **Keep it simple**: You don't need to perform long, complex routines to begin meditating (or possibly ever). Just a simple five minutes of quiet time can often bring dramatic results.

☐ **Easy does it**: Meditation shouldn't be a struggle. Be gentle with yourself. There is no right or wrong way to do it.

☐ **Get the habit**: The most important thing about meditation is to do it regularly, even if that's just a few minutes a day.

☐ **Do it for others**: Don't think you're being selfish by spending this time alone. Think about how a more peaceful, happier and calmer you will impact positively on the lives of all those around you.

☐ **On the move**: Look for opportunities to incorporate some simple meditation and mindfulness exercises into your ordinary daily routine, whether that's at work or out walking the dog.

☐ **Mix it up**: Meditation comes in all shapes and sizes. Try a few different techniques to see what suits you best.

☐ **Group therapy**: Although meditation is individual and highly portable, the effects can be even more powerful when taking part in a group session.

☐ **Stress free**: If you're stressed and having a bad day, or pushed for time, that's arguably the best time to take a break, breathe deeply and dip into a quiet, blissful meditative space.

Yoga Basics

☐ **Yoga is union:** Yoga is all about the union of the mind and body, to lift the student into higher levels of understanding and consciousness.

☐ **An ancient history:** The history of yoga can be traced back nearly 4,000 years, although it may date back even further, to prehistoric times.

☐ **Hatha Yoga:** Most forms of physical yoga in the West are some form of variation of traditional Hatha Yoga.

☐ **Six paths:** Hatha is one of the six yogic paths, which include following other, more spiritual and intellectual pursuits, as well as a physical practice.

☐ **The Yoga Sutras:** Patanjali was the first to document a written system of yoga technique and philosophy, in his Yoga Sutras.

☐ **Yamas and Niyamas:** These rules and guidelines for life give the yogi a code of conduct to follow, a list of what to do and what not to do.

☐ **Ashtanga Yoga:** Patanjali's Eight Limbs, otherwise known as Ashtanga Yoga – another popular yoga in the West – are a sequential movement through a yogi's life journey, like steps on a ladder.

☐ **The Holy Grail:** Samadhi is the final and ultimate goal, according to the Eight Limbs, where a yogi is set free and able to merge with the divine.

Getting Ready

☐ **Inside out**: Yoga can make you feel fabulous inside and out. The total mind and body workout, yoga will tone you up and calm you down.

☐ **Never too old**: Yoga is for everyone. You are never too old, too overweight, too inflexible to take up yoga.

☐ **Know your styles**: It's fun to experiment with yoga styles, so visit a new class whenever you can to mix things up a bit.

☐ **Born free**: You don't need any gear or kit to start yoga, just get to that first class and do it.

☐ **Portable yoga**: Yoga can be done anywhere and at any time. Learn a few postures and breathing exercises, then take them wherever you go.

☐ **Home space**: Allocate a small area of your home as your own private yoga studio. Light some candles, play some soothing music and away you go.

☐ **Healthy eating**: Start including more fruits and vegetables into your diet, and cut down on processed foods.

☐ **In the kitchen**: If you cook with raw ingredients at home, then you know exactly where your food has come from. No nasty surprises from processed factory foods.

The Postures

Sitting and Floor Postures

- [ ] Corpse Pose
- [ ] Child Pose
- [ ] Seated Staff Pose
- [ ] Easy Seated Pose
- [ ] Lion Pose
- [ ] Head-To-Knee Pose
- [ ] Seated Forward Bend
- [ ] Hero Pose
- [ ] Heron Pose
- [ ] Gate Pose
- [ ] Seated-Angle Pose
- [ ] Seated Side Stretch
- [ ] Cobbler's Pose

Standing Postures

- [ ] Mountain Pose
- [ ] Tree Pose
- [ ] Chair Pose
- [ ] Triangle Pose
- [ ] Half-Moon Pose
- [ ] Warrior Poses
- [ ] Extended-Angle Pose
- [ ] Wide-Legged Forward Bend
- [ ] Standing Forward Bend
- [ ] Single-Leg Forward Bend
- [ ] Eagle Pose
- [ ] Dancer's Pose

- [ ] Reclining Bound-Angle Pose
- [ ] Garland Pose
- [ ] Cow-Face Pose
- [ ] Sage Pose
- [ ] Lotus Posture
- [ ] Downward-Facing Dog Pose
- [ ] Plank Pose
- [ ] Four-Limbed Staff Pose

- [ ] Reclining Hero Pose
- [ ] Wheel Pose

Twists and Abdominal Toners

- [ ] Double Leg Raises
- [ ] Boat Pose
- [ ] Revolved Easy Pose
- [ ] Half Spinal Twist
- [ ] Revolved Abdomen Pose
- [ ] Pendant Pose

Back-Bending Postures

- [ ] Locust Pose
- [ ] Cobra Pose
- [ ] Upward-Facing Dog Pose
- [ ] Crocodile Pose
- [ ] Crescent-Moon Pose
- [ ] Frog Pose
- [ ] Camel Pose
- [ ] Easy Stretch Pose
- [ ] Bridge Pose
- [ ] Fish Pose

Arm Balances and Inverted Postures

- [ ] Crane Pose
- [ ] Inclined Plane Pose
- [ ] One-Hand-Over-Arm Balance
- [ ] Easy Inversion
- [ ] Hare Pose
- [ ] Plough Pose
- [ ] Shoulderstand
- [ ] Headstand
- [ ] Tripod Pose

Developing your Practice

☐ **Build a sequence to suit**: You can pick and choose your postures, being sure to include counter postures – forward and backward bends – to suit your individual needs.

☐ **Your 'go to' pose**: Any sequence should include Corpse Pose (page 88), for maximum relaxation and to give your body a chance to absorb the effects of your other postures.

☐ **What a way to start the day**: Performing a Sun Salutation in the morning, facing east, will energize you and give you an uplifting start to the day.

☐ **And to end the day**: Yoga can be performed at any time, but, as many postures can be energizing, concentrate on relaxation poses or meditation in the evening.

☐ **So much to choose from**: There are literally hundreds of postures, all conferring health benefits. See our lists on pages 210–12 to help you decide which best suit your needs.

☐ **Always remember**: Your yoga practice is personal to you. Try not to compare yourself to others who might have been practising for years. Keep in mind: 'Where I am right now is exactly where I need to be.'

☐ **Remember to smile**: There's a perception among some that yoga must be taken terribly seriously. It is a discipline but one that's designed to help you think and feel better.

☐ **Listen to your body**: If you can't smile through the pain and you feel a real twinge or uncomfortable stretch, ease off immediately.

Breath Control

☐ **Calm down**: Pranayama exercises are an excellent way to foster a greater sense of peace and calm in your life. They can also be invigorating, uplifting and energizing.

☐ **Life force**: Pranayama is much more than simply breathing. It is about drawing life force and nature's raw energy directly into your body.

☐ **Four stages**: There are four parts to the breath: inhalation, breath retention, exhalation and the pause after exhaling. All of these stages are important.

☐ **Multiple benefits**: Better breathing can provide an all-round boost for your body, easing away tensions and stress, and improving your general health and wellbeing.

☐ **Breathe and go**: Once you have learned a few simple pranayama breathing techniques, you can perform them wherever you go, whenever you are in need of a lift.

☐ **Beginner's luck**: Some yoga traditions call for certain postures and mudras (hand gestures) during pranayama, but this is not always necessary when you're starting out.

☐ **Peace out**: Pranayama, rather like meditation, can be integrated into a broader relaxation or stress-reduction programme.

☐ **Take a break**: If ever you start to feel dizzy during any of the exercises, stop and take a break.

Meditation

☐ **Keep it simple**: You don't need to perform long, complex routines to begin meditating (or possibly ever). Just a simple five minutes of quiet time can often bring dramatic results.

☐ **Easy does it**: Meditation shouldn't be a struggle. Be gentle with yourself. There is no right or wrong way to do it.

☐ **Get the habit**: The most important thing about meditation is to do it regularly, even if that's just a few minutes a day.

☐ **Do it for others**: Don't think you're being selfish by spending this time alone. Think about how a more peaceful, happier and calmer you will impact positively on the lives of all those around you.

☐ **On the move**: Look for opportunities to incorporate some simple meditation and mindfulness exercises into your ordinary daily routine, whether that's at work or out walking the dog.

☐ **Mix it up**: Meditation comes in all shapes and sizes. Try a few different techniques to see what suits you best.

☐ **Group therapy**: Although meditation is individual and highly portable, the effects can be even more powerful when taking part in a group session.

☐ **Stress free**: If you're stressed and having a bad day, or pushed for time, that's arguably the best time to take a break, breathe deeply and dip into a quiet, blissful meditative space.

Further Reading

Bender Birch, B., *Beyond Power Yoga*, Simon and Schuster, 2000

Brown, C., *The Yoga Bible: The Definitive Guide to Yoga Postures*, Godsfield Press, 2009

Chapman, J., *Yoga Therapies: 45 Sequences to Relieve Stress, Depression, Repetitive Strain, Sports Injuries and More*, Amorata Press, 2003

Chidvilasananda, S., *Yoga of Discipline*, 1996, SYDA Foundation

Desikachar, T.K.V., *The Heart of Yoga: Developing a Personal Practice*, Inner Traditions Bear and Company, 1999

Devi, V., *Yoga Sequences Companion: A Treasure Trove for Student and Teacher Alike*, Kool Kat Publications, 2012

Farhi, D., *Yoga Mind, Body and Spirit: A Return to Wholeness*, Henry Holt & Company Inc, 2000

Fraser, T., *Healthy Living: Yoga For You: A Step-by-Step Guide to Yoga at Home for Everybody*, Duncan Baird Publishers, 2008

Grime, L., *15-Minute Gentle Yoga: Get Real Results Anytime, Anywhere Four 15-minute workouts*, Dorling Kindersley, 2008

Iyengar, B.K.S., *B.K.S Iyengar Yoga, The Path to Holistic Health*, Dorling Kindersley, 2007

Iyengar, B.K.S., *Iyengar Yoga For Beginners*, Dorling Kindersley, 2006

Iyengar, B.K.S., *Light on Yoga: The Definitive Guide to Yoga Practice*, Thorsons, 2001

Kaminoff, L. and Matthews, A., *Yoga Anatomy: Second Edition*, Human Kinetics Publishers, 2011

Kirk, M. and Boon, B., *Hatha Yoga Illustrated*, Human Kinetics Europe Ltd, 2005

Lasatar, J., *Relax and Renew*, Rodmell Press, 2011

Long, R., *Key Poses of Yoga: Your Guide to Functional Anatomy in Yoga*, Independent Publisher, 2009

Massey, P., *Sports Pilates: How to Prevent and Overcome Sports Injuries*, Cico Books, 2011

McCall, T., *Yoga as Medicine: The Yogic Prescription for Health and Healing*, Bantam Books, 2012

Mohan, A. G., *Yoga Therapy: A Guide to the Therapeutic Use of Yoga and Ayurveda for Health and Fitness*, Shambhala Publications Inc, 2004

Pappas, S., *Yoga Posture Adjustments and Assisting: An Insightful Guide for Yoga Teachers and Students*, Trafford Publishing, 2005

Rosen, R., *The Yoga of Breath: A Step-by-Step Guide to Pranayama*. Shambhala Publications Inc, 2002

Schiffmann E., *Yoga: The Spirit and Practice of Moving Into Stillness*, Simon and Schuster, 1997

Sivananda Yoga Vedanta Centre, *Yoga: Your home practice companion*, Dorling Kindersley, 2009

Stephens, M., *Yoga Sequencing: Designing Transformative Yoga Classes*, North Atlantic Books. 2012

Townsend, N., *Yoga for Beginners: The Ultimate Guide to Getting Started*, CreateSpace Independent Publishing Platform, 2012

Websites

www.americanyogaassociation.org
The American Yoga Association offers a comprehensive guide to all that is yoga related.

www.britishmeditationsociety.org
A non-profit organization, which supports the teaching of meditation and its teachers across the UK.

www.bwywales.org.uk
The British Wheel of Yoga and its Welsh website offers retreats and information on teachers and classes in the area.

www.findyoga.com.au
Australia's largest yoga network includes a comprehensive directory of more than 2,000 studios and yoga classes across Australia and internationally.

www.harmonyyoga.co.uk
A great site if you're looking for a yoga teacher, a retreat, class or workshop in the UK.

http://life.gaiam.com
A great companion guide for those wanting to follow the yogic way of life, including recipes and how-to guides.

www.localyogaclasses.co.uk
An excellent website to help you find a yoga class in your local area, UK and ROI only.

www.myyogaonline.com
A comprehensive website that streams hundreds of yoga, meditation and related videos around the world, from beginner to advanced.

www.nhs.uk/Livewell/fitness/Pages/yoga.aspx
A very informative site if you're unsure if yoga is for you, you can take a look at what the medical community has to say about yoga.

www.omyogapages.com
An online forum that allows you to discuss yoga practice, keep a yoga journal and search for yoga retreats around the world.

www.swamij.com
An interesting website with articles concerning yoga, meditation and lifestyle; a great place for beginners to gain information.

www.wholeliving.com
A very well-organized and accessible site all about yoga and how to adapt it to your coordinated advice, with helpful and easy-to-follow tips and features.

www.yogaacrossamerica.org
A great website that aims to empower people across America to take up yoga, regardless of their background.

www.yogajournel.com
Lots of easy-to-follow instructions, plus some informative and inspiring articles about the art of yoga.

www.yogamad.com
A great site for those mad about having the correct yoga equipment, a comprehensive range of mats, bolsters and other yoga accessories.

www.yogamatters.com
A useful website with all the equipment you need to get started with yoga practice: mats, blocks, DVDs.

www.yogatoday.com
A very useful site for those needing a practitioner's help and advice, including the option to watch videos through paid membership only.

www.yogauk.com
A good place to find a yoga teacher in the UK.

www.yogaaustralia.org.au
Formally known as The Yoga Teachers Association of Australia, this website has great links for yoga teachers in Australia.

Index